TOOLS OF THE
ANCIENT
GREEKS

A Kid's Guide to the History & Science of Life in Ancient Greece

BUILD
inventions,
monuments,
and works of art

MEET
the people whose
ideas changed the
world

15
Hands-On
Activities

EXPLORE
the history of Greek
civilization with
hands-on activities

LEARN
how the discoveries
of ancient Greece
affect us today

Kris Bordessa

Photo and Image Credits

Cover images: Zvezda, Dave Scheel, Military Hobbies http://www.militaryhobbies.com
The Hoppin Painter, *Bell Krater* (mixing bowl) Photograph@2006 Museum of Fine Arts, Boston • Greek, South Italien, Late classical Period, about 380–370 BCE • Place of manufacture: Italy, Apulia • Ceramic, Red Figure • Height: 36.2 cm • Museum of Fine Arts, Boston • Gift of Alfred Ajami, Esther Anderson, Edith Bundy, Robert S. Czachor, Barbara and Lawrence A. Fleischman, Jonathan H. Kagan, Bruce and Ingrid McAlpine, Josephine L. Murray, Robin Symes, and Catherine C. Vermeule. 1988.532

Illustrations: by Shawn Braley unless otherwise noted.

Pg. 1: Grecian Mask: Cheryl Ronstad; Pg. 4, 119, 122: Maps from Bernard SUZANNE's web site 'Plato and his Dioalogues', http://plato-dialogues.org; Pg. 26: Gaea relief: Courtesy of members.tripod.com/ ~ Poseidon64/pics.html; Pg. 34: Theatre of Dionysus: Courtesy of www.winterscapes.com/dionysus/theatre.htm; Pg. 37: Papyrus Note; Courtesy of Alain Jacquesson Director of the Bibliothèque Publique et Universitaire, Geneva, Switzerland; Pg. 50: Sacrifice to Gods: http://www.lavistachurchofchrist.org; Pg. 51: Heracles: Copyright Artis Opus Gallery 2003/Photo by Michael A. Sikora; Pg. 67: Seated man with head on fist: http://serp.la.asu.edu/; Pgs. 82–86: Temple of Artemis; Colossus of Rhodes; Lighthouse at Alexandria: Computer visualizations by Bill Munns; Pgs. 111–112: Andromeda; Orion; Boast of Cassiopeia: Courtesy of NASA and STScI.

Nomad Press
A division of Nomad Communications
10 9 8 7 6 5 4 3 2
Copyright © 2006 by Nomad Press
All rights reserved.

ISBN: 0-9749344-6-4
Questions regarding the ordering of this book should be addressed to
Independent Publishers Group
814 N. Franklin St.
Chicago, IL 60610
www.ipgbook.com

Nomad Press
2456 Christian St.
White River Junction, VT 05001
www.nomadpress.net

Contents

Other titles from Nomad Press

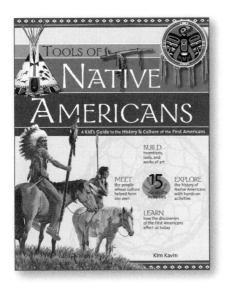

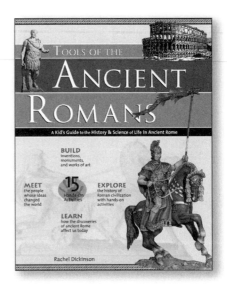

INTRODUCTION

WHEN WE LOOK AT THE MODERN WORLD AND TRY TO figure out why we live the way we do, we find ourselves turning again and again to a small nation in the Mediterranean Sea, and to events that took place there more than 2,000 years ago.

Much of the world around us has been heavily influenced by people we now call ancient Greeks. If you find that hard to believe, just look to the sky. Our constellations go by names like Orion, Cassiopeia, Andromeda, and Perseus. Those names come directly from ancient Greek mythology. Even one of America's space programs was named for the Greek god, Apollo.

Some American cities sport Greek names— Athens, Georgia, is one and Homer, Alaska, is another. Some of our most famous buildings feature sweeping colonnades and imposing columns. These elements were prominent in ancient Greek architecture. The Lincoln Memorial in Washington, D.C., is just one example—it was modeled after the Greek Parthenon.

From our democratic society to our theater, and from our architecture to our names for constellations, ancient Greek culture has influenced our lives today.

When we measure, map, and mold the world, we use tools that were invented by the ancient Greeks. Even when we do something simple like argue or run a race, we have the ancient Greeks to thank for showing us how to do it best.

Tools of the Ancient Greeks will take you through the intellectual triumphs and mechanical creations of this long-gone, but not-forgotten civilization and show how their world has influenced ours. Biology, astronomy, athletics, democracy, logic, and reason—the Greeks laid the groundwork in nearly every field of learning you can imagine. With this book you can follow in their footsteps.

BCE? CE?

As you read, you will notice dates with the letters BCE. This stands for Before Common Era. The beginning of the Common Era is marked by the birth of Jesus and begins with the year 1 followed by the letters CE. Events that occurred before the first year of the Common Era are classified as Before Common Era. The years BCE may seem backward, because as time passes, the years actually become smaller in number. A child born in 300 BCE, for instance, would celebrate his or her 10th birthday in the year 290 BCE. Think of it as a countdown to Common Era.

Ancient Greece
and the Beginnings of Democracy

WHEN WE TALK ABOUT ANCIENT GREECE, WE ARE referring to the time period from about 800 BCE to 31 BCE. Those 800 years produced some amazing ideas, inventions, discoveries, and beliefs. We use many of them in our daily lives today. But before we focus on those clever Greeks, let's take a quick look at how ancient Greece evolved.

The First Greeks

Situated on the Aegean Sea, ancient Greece is considered part of the Aegean world. The Aegean world includes all of the civilizations in this area. The Minoans were the first great civilization in the Aegean world. They lived a peaceful existence on the island of Crete, near mainland Greece.

Archaeologists have unearthed Minoan palaces with elegant rooms and elaborate wall paintings. The Minoan culture was wealthy. The Minoans traded with other populations throughout the Aegean world, including the Egyptians, but archaeologists and historians can't find any evidence that the Minoans had an army, or even soldiers.

Around 1450 BCE the island of Crete and the Minoans fell under the power of people called the Mycenaeans. The Mycenaeans lived on the mainland of Greece. They were excellent

A Minoan.

A Mycenaean.

craftspeople. They built elaborate underground tombs, giant defensive walls, and the Lion Gate that still stands today.

Like the Minoans, the Mycenaeans were traders. They traded items such as animal skins and oil. But unlike the peaceful Minoans, the Mycenaeans were a warlike people. The most famous Mycenaean battle of all is one you'll hear more about later: the battle of Troy in the Trojan War.

The mighty Mycenaeans fell under attack between 1200 and 1150 BCE. In less than one hundred years the Mycenaeans abandoned their civilization, leaving few clues as to how they lived. This time period (from about 1100 to 800 BCE) is known as the Greek dark age because all written language and signs of culture completely disappeared. Most historians think that those who survived the upheaval settled into an agricultural, almost tribal, way of life.

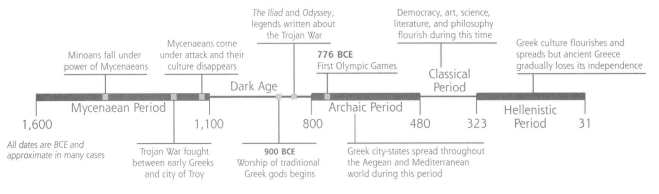

The age of the Mycenaeans is described in two of the most famous stories in all of literature: Homer's *Iliad* and *Odyssey*. These famous poems tell stories about the Mycenaean civilization and give us some idea of what life must have been like before the Greek dark age.

> **There weren't any Greeks in ancient Greece. That term was given to the people of Greece generations later by the Romans. The people we now know as ancient Greeks called themselves Hellenes, after Helen of Troy. Hellenic means Greek.**

Around 800 BCE, small agricultural communities slowly expanded into larger settlements. These settlements extended from mainland Greece, across islands scattered throughout the Aegean Sea, and to Asia Minor. This peninsula of land across the Aegean Sea from mainland Greece is what we now know as Turkey. Greek colonies even developed in areas that are now Italy, Spain, and Egypt. Ancient Greece covered a lot of ground, but it wasn't a single country with one ruler or government like it is today. Instead, those small settlements became a collection of more than 1,000 isolated city-states, called poleis.

The Trojan Horse.

words to know

> **archaeologist:** someone who studies the tools, buildings, graves, and other objects of people who lived in the past to learn about their culture.
>
> **polis:** city-state (plural *poleis*).
>
> **acropolis:** high place of the city.

Greek *Poleis*

A typical city-state, called a **polis**, was made up of a central town surrounded by smaller villages and agricultural lands. The central towns were built around a hill called an **acropolis**. The acropolis was fortified against wartime attacks and offered a clear view of attackers as well as protection to the citizens.

Know Your Ancient Greeks: Helen

According to legend, Helen was the most beautiful woman in the world. She was the daughter of the Greek god, Zeus, and a mortal queen, Leda. Men came from all over ancient Greece hoping to marry the Spartan princess. Helen had to obey the wishes of her mortal father, Tyndarecus, and she married a man named Menelaus, king of Sparta.

The goddess Aphrodite had other plans for Helen. Aphrodite was in debt to a man named Paris because he had chosen her as the most beautiful of three women in a contest. In payment, Aphrodite offered up the beautiful Helen to Paris, and made Paris so attractive that Helen wouldn't be able to refuse him. While Menelaus was away, Paris charmed Helen. People debate whether Paris kidnapped Helen or she ran away with him, but in any case, Menelaus was not happy.

When Paris and Helen reached Troy, they were married. Menelaus and his brother, Agamemnon, followed with an army of men to retrieve Helen. And that's how the Trojan War began in about 1200 BCE.

Each city-state had its own traditions and government. Ancient Greece, therefore, was not one country, but a bunch of tiny nations.

The period in ancient Greece from 800 to 500 BCE is called the **archaic** period. During this time many city-states were ruled by king-like figures known as the **basileus**. People soon tired of this type of leadership and overthrew these rulers. It was within these city-states that the first democratic government was tested.

A New Kind of Government

Like most ancient Greek city-states in the archaic period, **Athens** was ruled by a king. A council of nobles, called the **Areopagus**, served under the Athenian king. As Athens thrived, the nobles grew richer, gaining money, land, and power. As the members of the Areopagus grew more powerful, the king lost power. Over time, Athens evolved into an **oligarchy**, meaning "rule by a few."

Greek king or basileus.

From around 700 to 500 BCE, Athens was ruled by an oligarchy, but since the rulers were wealthy aristocrats, the common people grew more and more frustrated. As the people became more vocal about their complaints, most oligarchies were gradually replaced by a **democracy**. In about 500 BCE, democracy became the favored form of government. This early democracy was a step in the right direction, but it didn't allow all citizens to participate—only free, male citizens were allowed to take part in government decisions.

AREOPAGUS—APPOINTS ARCHONS AND HAS FINAL SAY ON ALL MATTERS OF STATE

9 ARCHONS—TO RUN THE CITY-STATE

In Athens, the Areopagus, not the people, elected nine rulers, called "**archons**," to run the city-state. But the archons couldn't make a decision without the approval of the Areopagus, so the Areopagus had the final word. Archons ruled for one year, and met weekly to discuss things like taxes, and war. Commoners were allowed to attend the assembly to speak out about a case—as long as they were male.

words to know

archaic: from a much earlier period of time, the earliest phases of a culture.

basileus: a Greek king.

Athens: the cultural center of ancient Greece .

Areopagus: a council of nobles beneath the king.

oligarchy: rule by a few.

democracy: rule by the people .

archon: after the age of kings, city-states were ruled by nine archons.

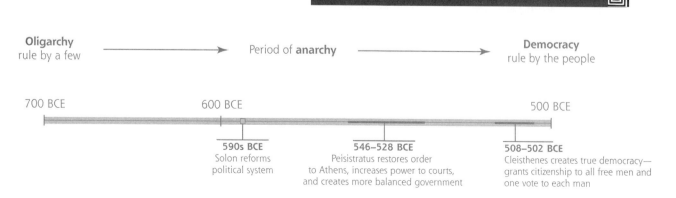

Oligarchy rule by a few	Period of **anarchy**		Democracy rule by the people

700 BCE	600 BCE		500 BCE
	590s BCE Solon reforms political system	**546–528 BCE** Peisistratus restores order to Athens, increases power to courts, and creates more balanced government	**508–502 BCE** Cleisthenes creates true democracy— grants citizenship to all free men and one vote to each man

Because the archons were appointed by the wealthy, things were still unfair for the common people. While wheat farmers struggled to grow successful crops, the vineyards and olive groves thrived. Guess who owned many of those? The wealthy men of the Areopagus! While the men of the Areopagus sold their wine and olive oil and became richer, the wheat farmers—who couldn't provide enough wheat for Athens—grew poorer and poorer. In order to pay off their debts, poor wheat farmers were forced to sell their wives and children (and sometimes even themselves) into slavery.

In Athens, groups of poor and middle-class citizens complained about the way their city-state was run. They demanded to be given some power to make laws. In 594 BCE the Areopagus recognized that the people were ready to revolt.

Solon.

Homer's *Iliad* and *Odyssey*

The Iliad tells the story of a single event that occurred during the ninth year of the Trojan War. Achilles, a Greek warrior, became angry at the Greek leader Agamemnon when Agamemnon took a slave who belonged to Achilles. In retaliation, Achilles withdrew from battle and prayed that the war would turn against the Greeks—and it did. Achilles finally returned to battle when his best friend was killed by the great Trojan hero, Hector.

In the *Odyssey*, Homer tells of Odysseus's long journey home after the Trojan War. Delayed for 10 years by the gods, Odysseus encounters much trouble on the way and falls in love with the goddess Kalypso. But when given the choice between staying with Kalypso and becoming immortal, or returning to his wife who is waiting at home, Odysseus chooses to continue home.

Agamemnon.

words to know

boule: a government council of 400 men balancing the Areopagus.

legislative bill: the action of proposing a law, an idea for a new law.

It agreed to give all political power to one man, a wealthy businessman and aristocrat named Solon.

The government of Athens needed to provide more rights and protection for the common people. As a first step in this direction, Solon abolished slavery caused by debt. A man didn't have to sell his wife or children to pay off money he owed any longer!

Solon was one of the Seven Wise Men of ancient Greece. Today *solon* means a man who is a respected leader.

Solon then created four groups of citizens. Members of the wealthiest two groups were allowed to serve on the Areopagus. Another group was allowed to serve on the "**boule**," an elected council. The boule was made up of 400 men and served as a kind of balance to the Areopagus. Members of the boule were elected and could only serve for one year.

A fourth group, made up of the poorest people, could participate in an assembly. Between 4,000 and 6,000 men attended each assembly. This assembly acted as the voice of the people and had a lot of power.

The council made recommendations about laws and state business, kind of like **legislative bills** today. The assembly discussed these recommendations and voted on them. The men of the assembly voted to elect officials, declare war, grant citizenship, and spend public funds. The assembly had direct authority in affairs of the state and the council enforced the decisions made by the assembly.

Democracy

The word *democracy* comes from the Greek term for "people's rule." Democracy allows all the people of a governed body to vote on matters of importance, allowing the voice of the majority to be heard. Ancient Greece gave the world its first experiments in democracy, and although these experiments lasted less than 200 years, the lessons learned more than 2,000 years ago have had a major impact on most of today's governments around the world.

AREOPAGUS—MEMBERS OF THE WEALTHIEST TWO GROUPS

BOULE—ELECTED COUNCIL

ASSEMBLY—POOREST GROUP OF CITIZENS

Greek Justice

People accused of a crime in ancient Greece were subject to the judgment of a jury of their **peers**. Each year, 6,000 men were chosen to act as jurors, though not all of them sat on the same jury at the same time. These large juries made it nearly impossible for anyone to bribe the jury and influence the verdict. Jurors were selected by drawing lots and had to be least 30 years old. They were paid a daily fee for their service. The courts were kept in order by a **magistrate** and the jurors usually voted twice: once to determine guilt or innocence and a second time to decide upon the penalty. The majority ruled, and there was no such thing as an appeal—the jurors' word was final.

These changes got the common people more involved in politics, but didn't eliminate their complaints entirely. Solon left and Athens fell into **anarchy**, a chaotic period with no clear leader. Twice during this chaotic time a man named Peisistratus tried to take over, but twice he failed.

Out Among the Citizens

American presidents like to visit factories, farms, daycare centers, and schools to find out what the "person on the street" thinks about the government's actions. More than 2,000 years ago, Greek leaders did the very same thing. Around 550 BCE, for example, our old friend Peisistratus often inspected the farms and country homes of his subjects. One day, after he had made a new tax on the income of farmers, he came across a farmer digging in a field of stones and asked what his income was. The farmer replied, "Just so many aches and pains, and of these pains, Peisistratus ought to take his 10 percent in taxes." Peisistratus was so surprised by the farmer's honesty that he gave the farmer a refund on all the taxes he had paid.

Assembly Duty

Many men had to travel from the countryside to the city of Athens to participate in the assembly. Sometimes, not enough men showed up. When this happened, a band of specially trained slaves went looking for those who had shirked their duty. Men who had neglected to show up at the assembly were swatted with a rope dipped in red paint and forced to pay a fine.

Finally, Peisistratus successfully took charge of Athens in 546 BCE and worked to restore order. He decided to turn Athens into a city of culture. He built new buildings and invited artists and poets to come to Athens.

He kept the constitution that Solon introduced and increased the power of the courts that benefited the lower classes. As poor Greek citizens became more involved in the government by acting as assemblymen or jurors, the aristocrats were forced into a smaller role on the political stage, creating a more balanced government.

Peisistratus died around 528 BCE, and his son Hippias took over. Hippias was not a good leader and when Athens was attacked by **Sparta** in 510 BCE, Hippias escaped to Persia.

Cleisthenes is important because, from 508 to 502 BCE, he helped create the world's first successful democracy. He granted citizenship to all free men living in Athens and **Attica**, and formed a council and assembly that allowed those citizens to actively participate in government. "One man, one vote" became the guiding principle—a belief that still holds in today's democracies.

Hippias, son of Peisistratus.

words to know

peer: a person who is of equal standing with another in a group: your friends are your peers.

magistrate: someone who administers laws.

anarchy: a chaotic period with no clear leader.

Sparta: a warlike city-state in ancient Greece.

Attica: Athens and the surrounding region.

Greek wrestlers.

Athens

While each city-state in ancient Greece was governed by its own people by the time of Cleisthenes's rule, Athens emerged as the prime example of democracy. For the first time in history, people had the ability to publicly voice their opinions and be heard.

This freedom to think and share opinions spurred not only a democratic government but also a desire for knowledge. Athens was filled with scholars, artists, scientists, and philosophers—people wondering "how" and "why." Works by famous poets, philosophers, and mathematicians filled huge libraries. Artists carved great marble sculptures. Architects erected grand buildings.

Away With You!

Another powerful change in the new democratic system of Athens was the introduction of ostracism—a kind of "reverse election" in which voters could decide to kick a citizen out of town for 10 years.

First, citizens voted whether ostracism should take place. If this vote passed, each citizen would then write the name of the person they wanted to banish on *ostraca*, fragments of broken pottery. If more than 6,000 citizens participated in this second vote, then the person whose name appeared most often would be banished.

This practice was a powerful threat against wealthy aristocrats who were considered dangerous or untrustworthy. If you bothered too many people with your actions, they'd get together and legally boot you out!

At the end of the fifth century, this system changed so that people accused of wrongdoing were judged by a jury of their peers. The typical jury had several hundred people on it.

One of These Democracies Is Not Like the Other

While Athens had the first democratic government, its democracy was far different from what we have in the United States today. To begin with, while all citizens could serve in the government, few of the people who lived in Athens were actually considered citizens!

Women, for example, were not citizens. Slaves and most foreigners were not allowed to become citizens, and male adults could only become citizens if both of their parents were from Athens. These restrictions meant that out of an estimated population of 250,000, only about 30,000 were actual citizens. Keep in mind, though, that the United States started its democracy in much the same way. Women couldn't vote in the United States until 1920. Slaves counted as only three-fifths of a person—and the slave owner (not the slave) got to use the vote! If Athenian democracy had lasted, perhaps it would have evolved as the United States's has. But Greek democracy lasted less than 200 years, ending around 338 BCE, when the Greek world lost its independence.

Another difference is in how government officials were selected. The United States has a representative government. Citizens decide to run for office, then we vote for one of these people to represent us. In Athens, your name was submitted with all the others and you might be "elected" to serve. Serving wasn't an option, it was a duty. If you refused to participate, you lost your civil rights and were shunned by others.

With regular wars, the citizen soldiers of Athens could be called upon at any time to go to battle. Men kept themselves in good shape by participating regularly in rigorous sporting events such as wrestling, boxing, and chariot racing.

Sparta

Things were different in Sparta, another powerful city-state in ancient Greece. Sparta's economy was based on slave labor. As the slave population grew, so did the threat of a slave revolt, so Spartans had to keep their slaves in check. These slaves, called helots, were monitored closely by the Spartans and treated cruelly. It was a rite of passage for those in training for war to stalk and kill helots, who must have lived in constant fear.

Coins in Ancient Greece

Each city-state had its own coins, recognizable by a distinctive design. Coins were stamped to indicate how much metal they contained, and the markings on both sides of the coin helped to ensure that people wouldn't "shave" it to collect bits of the valuable metal.

A silver coin of the Seleucid king Antiochus IV.

The Spartans saw militaristic life as a way for men to reach their full potential. Because the men of Sparta spent all of their time striving for militaristic perfection, they were always ready for war. They developed and practiced complicated maneuvers designed to surprise enemies on the battlefield.

Spartans practiced moving in the dark without the aid of torches, and Spartan men spent all day practicing to be soldiers. The women and slaves took care of the daily chores necessary for the city-state to survive.

Spartans were ruthless in their quest to produce fine soldiers. Boys were taken from their mothers at the age of seven to begin military training. Boys became soldiers at age 20.

Sparta never achieved the democratic ideals of Athens. It was ruled by a military oligarchy during times of war and a senate of 30 in between wars. Sparta did contribute to the rise of democracy and culture in Athens though, by helping to defend all of the Greek world from Persian invaders in the sixth century BCE. Without Sparta, Athens could not have flourished. In the end Sparta was also responsible for the decline of Athens in the fourth century BCE, as the two city-states battled each other in war after war.

Spartan soldier.

Farming, Trade,

and the Greek Way of Life

AT THE HEIGHT OF ANCIENT GREEK CIVILIZATION, THERE were an estimated 250,000 people living in Athens alone. The area surrounding Athens—called Attica—was home to another 250,000. While Athens was a bustling city-state, life in the countryside was quiet and slow-paced. The people in the countryside were conservative, which means they liked things to stay the way they had always been.

The people who lived in Attica were mostly farmers, raising crops in the open countryside. The farmers of Attica viewed the Athenians as lazy and frivolous with their money. Athenians, with the educated and worldly ways, considered farmers to be old-fashioned, dim-witted, and miserly. But Athenians depend-

ed upon farmers to supply their city with food, and the farmers of Attica needed the city people to buy it.

Farmers worked hard, from daybreak to sunset, growing and harvesting the food that would feed their families. What the farmer didn't need for his own table was sold to the Athenians at the **agora.**

GREECE

Attica

Thebes
Boeotia
Tanagra
Oropus
Asopus
Oropia
Euboea
EURIPUS STRAITS
GULF OF CORINTH
Megaris
Corinth
Corinth
BAY OF ELEUSIS
Salamis
SARONIC GULF
Aegina
Aegina
Epidaurus

The Agora

At the heart of each city-state was the agora. This busy place was the economic, religious, and cultural center for the region. Every day, farmers and local craftspeople set up stalls filled with their wares. Think of the agora as an ancient version of a supermarket. Farmers came from the surrounding countryside to sell fruits and vegetables, cheese, wine, and meat. Fishermen displayed fish fresh from the Aegean Sea. Craftspeople offered pottery, hardware, and books to passersby.

The men of the community came to the agora every morning to purchase the day's food for their families. This gave them the opportunity to gather with other men from the community to hear the news or discuss politics. Shopping for food in ancient Greece was not just a necessity, it was a social activity!

Surrounding the bustling activity of the agora you might find several temples, army headquarters, a court of law, a notice board with information about upcoming legal cases and new laws, and a prison.

From Fruit to Wine

The grape harvest meant an abundance of fruit to be made into wine. Winemakers filled big containers with the ripe, sweet-smelling grapes, then a man would step right into the middle of the container and use his feet to crush them! As the grapes were stomped, the juice was released and accumulated in the bottom of the container. The juice was then separated from the grape stems and pulp. This was hard work—40 pounds of grapes might only yield 1 or 2 gallons of juice! Once the juice was extracted, it was ready for the **fermentation** process, which could take another year or more. Making wine required lots of patience.

Food for Thought

The life of a farmer in ancient Greece wasn't easy. The land was rugged and much of it was too steep for farmers to cultivate **crops**. Farmers **terraced** the land to make more usable space by creating big steps in the hillsides. Even in areas where the land was level, the soil was rocky and poor. To make matters worse, the **climate** of Greece is extremely **arid**. But people must eat, so farmers toiled to produce what food they could, cultivating crops that would thrive in tough conditions.

Grapes, olives, and figs were the primary crops in ancient Greece. Other crops were grown as well, but weren't very important to the ancient Greek diet. Chickens and goats were raised to provide milk, cheese, and eggs.

words to know

agora: open-air market.

fermentation: a process where something breaks down into a simpler substance.

crop: plants grown for food or other uses.

terraced: strips of level land cut into a hillside.

climate: typical weather in an area.

arid: very dry, with little rainfall.

trade: exchanging one thing for another.

export: to sell to another country.

The majority of the grape crop was turned into wine. Olives, too, were turned into a liquid product. Olive oil was used for cooking, as you might expect, and also as fuel for lamps, in beauty products, and as a soap of sorts, to remove dirt from the body.

Trade

Bread was important to the ancient Greek diet, though wheat grew poorly. Farmers had greater success with barley, which was more tolerant of the tough conditions, and used it for making barley bread. Even so, farmers could not produce a sufficient amount of grain to fill the needs of the country, making **trade** essential. Greek merchant ships were loaded with **exports** of wine, olive oil, silver, and pottery sent to trade across the Mediterranean and Aegean Seas.

What About Pirates?

When trading ships ventured out to sea, they were at risk of being attacked by pirates. To combat this problem, Greek merchant ships were equipped with bow rams to fight off pirate ships. Projecting underwater from the bow of the ship, the copper-tipped ram could punch holes in enemy ships that came too close, causing the ships to sink. It was rare for people to learn how to swim during ancient times—even for sailors who spent most of their time on the open ocean. Because of this, causing a ship to sink was quite effective. The pirates on board would quickly perish as they found themselves in the water, unable to stay afloat.

They even ventured into the Black Sea to trade. Goods from Egypt, Libya, Cyprus, Sicily, and Italy made their way back to ancient Greece on these ships. Athens **imported** metals, furs, and grain.

The merchant ships were less than 100 feet long and graced with a single rectangular sail. The sail was used when winds were favorable—otherwise the ship was powered by men rowing in unison. The ships were open, with no place for the crew to escape wind, rain, and splashing waves. Because of the dangers of traveling in a vessel such as this, crews seldom left sight of land and would pull the ship onto shore at night or if seas became too rough.

Counting Cash

Tradespeople used a system called **barter** to make sure that each trade was fair. They set certain values on their goods, and in order for a trade to be considered fair, they needed to receive something of equal value. The earliest coins were probably lumps of

Q: What **ingredient** did ancient Greeks use in place of **wheat** to make **bread**?

metal stamped to reveal the metal's weight. These coins may have been given as pay to soldiers or used in trade. The coin's recipient could use the metal to purchase goods.

Around 600 BCE, Aegina, a city-state near Athens, made the first Greek coin that could be used as payment for goods. Around 590 BCE Athens issued a coin made of silver called a drachma. Imprinted with an owl, which was recognized as Athena's symbol, drachmas were the most common currency in the Aegean world during the height of the Athenian empire.

Thales (*circa* 636–*circa* 546 BCE)

An ancient Greek famous for being a deep thinker, Thales put his knowledge to practical use as well. When he was mocked for thinking all the time and never working, he said, "Anyone can make money if he puts his mind to it." His friends challenged him to prove it.

To do so, Thales first had to decide on the best way to make money. In the sixth century BCE, olive oil was such a necessity that he thought olives looked like the best bet. He learned as much as he could about the growing, harvesting, and pressing of olives to make oil. He discovered that olive production had been down for the past few years, which led him to investigate weather patterns. The previous few seasons had produced very poor crops, but Thales predicted a change in the weather for the upcoming season that would mean a heavy crop.

Thales toured the olive groves and purchased all the oil presses he could from the discouraged growers. The presses had been almost useless recently, so growers were happy to sell them.

When the weather was favorable the following year, olive trees produced a huge crop. All the presses belonged to Thales. He had created a **monopoly**, and olive farmers who wanted to make oil were forced to pay a fee to borrow Thales's presses. This monopoly—and Thales's thinking—brought him great wealth.

Olive press.

Around 550 BCE, three drachmas might buy a bushel of grain, and a sheep was worth eight drachmas. The daily wage for a laborer was about one drachma. Some historians estimate that a family of four could live for four days on a single drachma.

Only Sparta rejected the drachma, preferring to stick with the more familiar heavy metal lumps. This likely discouraged trade between Sparta and other city-states in ancient Greece. It wasn't until sometime in the third century BCE that Sparta finally began to **mint** coins.

As coinage became more common, most city-states minted their own coins, decorating them with eagles, owls, horses, and **mythological** creatures like Pegasus, the winged horse. Coins made in Athens wouldn't necessarily be accepted in, say, Aegina. To deal with this problem, money changers called *trapezitai* would set up tables in agoras and other public places. Visitors from different city-states could go to the *trapezitai* and exchange their coins for coins of equal value.

When Alexander the Great conquered much of Asia in the 300s BCE, he spread the use of one Greek currency across the land. This made it much easier for people to trade as they traveled through different city-states. For a time, the drachma fell out of favor. The modern state of Greece reissued the drachma in 1832, and it was used until 2002, when Greece joined other European countries in adopting the euro.

Currant Events

One type of dried fruit favored by the ancient Greeks was the currant. Currants are dried fruits, quite like raisins, only smaller. Ancient Greeks called them Corinths, after the polis where they originated. Over the years, the term evolved to currants—a name we still use today. Your can buy currants at the supermarket.

What Was the Food Like?

Athenians ate two substantial meals per day. Their light lunch was called *ariston*, and dinner was called *deipnon*. Meat was eaten only a couple of times each week, and this was likely fresh fish, rabbit, deer, or pigeon. Meat was more commonly available in rural areas, as people had access to hunting and space to raise animals. In towns and cities, meat and fish were available at the agora.

Grains, fruits, and vegetables were the main part of the ancient Greek diet. Breakfast might simply be a piece of bread dipped in wine. Lunch might be bread with cheese, olives, figs, dates, grapes, or currants. Supper was usually something like a thick porridge made from barley. Vegetables such as peas, garlic, lettuce, parsley, mushrooms, artichokes, or beets might accompany the porridge. While today's tables are almost always set with forks, spoons, and knives, the ancient Greeks considered it proper to eat with their fingers. For messier meals, a piece of flat bread might be used as a spoon.

words to know

import: to buy from another country.

barter: to trade one thing for another.

monopoly: to control all of something in a market.

mint: to make coins.

mythological: imaginary.

Snack Like a Greek

Some foods that were prepared by ancient Greeks are still common today. The ancient Greeks rolled pastry as thin as leaves to make Spanakopita, or spinach pie, and baklava. They coined the term phyllo (or leaf) for their super-thin pastry, because it was as thin as leaves. Spinach pie may not sound like something you'd like to try, but baklava is a dessert made with phyllo, honey, and nuts. You can try baklava for yourself—see the recipe at the end of this chapter.

Another Greek food that you may recognize is feta cheese. The name *feta* (or sliced) was given to the cheese in the seventeenth century, but the history of this cheese goes back to the time of Homer. Feta cheese is special because it is made only from goat's or sheep's milk. According to legend, Polyphemus, the Cyclopes who imprisoned Odysseus (you'll read more about him in later chapters) is said to have been the first manufacturer of feta cheese, quite by accident. He stored sheep's milk from his flock in animal skin bags. One day he discovered that some bags that he had left for a number of days were not full of liquid as he expected, but a firm mass of creamy cheese.

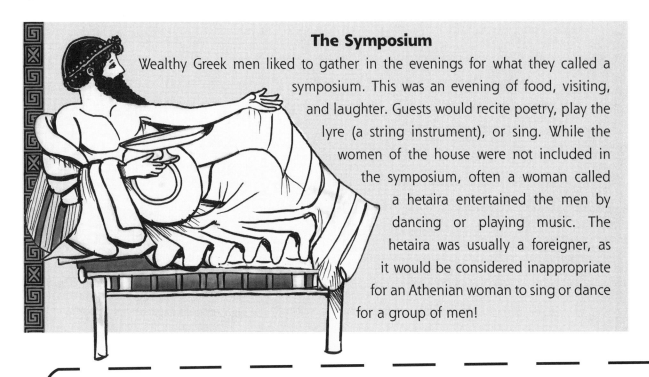

The Symposium

Wealthy Greek men liked to gather in the evenings for what they called a symposium. This was an evening of food, visiting, and laughter. Guests would recite poetry, play the lyre (a string instrument), or sing. While the women of the house were not included in the symposium, often a woman called a hetaira entertained the men by dancing or playing music. The hetaira was usually a foreigner, as it would be considered inappropriate for an Athenian woman to sing or dance for a group of men!

activity: Host Your Own Symposium

Invite a group of friends to join you for an afternoon with an ancient Greek feel. In order to host your own symposium, you'll need to provide food, drinks, and entertainment. Here are a few ideas.

1 Send an invitation written on a scroll. Make sure to ask your friends to bring a favorite poem or short story to share. You can even suggest that they come in costume! The ancient Greeks wore simple tunics made of linen. Your guests can drape themselves with a white sheet.

2 The ancient Greeks lounged on couches called *klines* during their symposiums. Since you might not have enough couches for your guests, lay towels and pillows on the floor in a circle.

Summertime meals were prepared outside over an open fire. In the wintertime, a small stove called a brazier was used indoors for both cooking and heating the home. Houses had a small hole in the roof to allow smoke to escape.

One special ancient Greek dish you are probably familiar with is an egg omelet. The Greeks filled theirs with cheese, honey, and sheep's brains.

> **Chill Out**
> The ancient Greeks preferred their drinks chilled, so they stored their beverages in containers underground. While this worked reasonably well, those who could afford it used ice, which mule trains hauled from the mountains into the city every day.

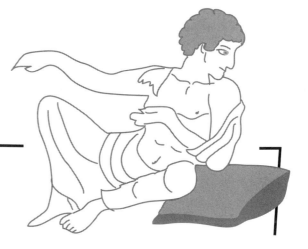

3 Teach your guests about proper symposium behavior. It was considered bad form to drop a cup or laugh during a prayer, tap or whistle to music, or spit across the table at the wine pourer.

4 Small tidbits of food were served because they were easy to pick up with only one hand. Offer your symposium guests grapes, cubes of cheese, and small slices of bread. The ancient Greeks drank wine—you can serve grape juice.

5 For entertainment, ask each guest to share their favorite poem or short story with the group. You might have a book of poems on hand, in case some guests forget to bring a favorite. If one of your guests is a musician, ask him or her to perform.

6 Try playing a game similar to one played at ancient Greek symposiums. Choose a poem or nursery rhyme that is familiar to everyone. The first player should recite the first line. Going around the circle, each player adds a line from memory. See how far you can go!

Rules of Relief

Even though it was acceptable for men to relieve themselves out of doors, they had to be careful not to offend the gods. Hesiod, an early Greek poet, gave this advice:

"Do not urinate standing upright facing the sun but remember to do it either when the sun has set or when it is rising. Do not make water either on the road or beside the road as you go along and do not bare yourself. The nights belong to the blessed gods. A good man who has a wise heart sits or goes to the wall of an enclosed court."

Bathing, etc.

The earliest bathtubs in ancient Greece were built by the Mycenaeans at the Palace of Nestor at Pylos and were made from **terra-cotta**. The ancient Greeks kept themselves exceptionally clean. Many homes were equipped with a bath—a room that may have contained a terra-cotta tub as well as a basin that sat on a small table, used for washing hands and face. Some of the wealthier homes may even have had showers similar to those found in public bathhouses, with water piped in to spray on bathers.

Water came to the city of Athens via terra-cotta pipes that fed public fountains. People carried empty vessels to the fountain, filled them with water, and carried them home. Dirty water was usually just dumped outside, along with the other trash that people generated. Rubbish was often piled ankle deep along roadways, making conditions in ancient Greece less than sanitary.

Human waste, too, was a problem. There were no public toilets, but it was common for men to relieve themselves in public. With so many people in the city, the streets quickly filled with smelly waste. Dung collectors worked to

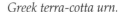

Greek terra-cotta urn.

24

clean up the mess, but by law could not dump the waste within half a mile of the city. Hauling waste that far was time consuming, and limited the amount of dung that could be removed each day.

Ancient Greeks depended on clay jars to collect their toilet waste. Slaves disposed of the waste in these stinky jars as part of their job.

It's a Man's World

The male head of a wealthy family enforced household rules, controlled the family money, and arranged for the education of his children. His family—wife, children, and slaves—were called *oikos*, meaning "household. The head of the household spent much of his time in town, educating himself or practicing his athletic skills, and the daily running of the home was usually left to his wife.

Women from wealthy families in Athens were expected to supervise the household slaves. The slaves did most of the housework, cared for small children, and took care of certain tasks, such as spinning and weaving.

Wealthy women lived, for the most part, separately from all men who were not part of their *oikos*, seldom even speaking to them. Women and female children were confined to their homes except for special occasions, such as weddings and funerals. When the man of the house entertained his friends, women and girls were expected to retire to the women's quarters, since it was considered inappropriate for them to mix with men who were not family members.

In ancient Greece if you weren't wealthy, you were likely poor and struggling to put food on the table. Women from poor families or slaves couldn't afford the luxury of staying indoors. They were needed to help fetch water, sell wares at the marketplace, or harvest crops. Some poor women worked for pay—weaving, harvesting grapes, or even nursing babies for wealthier women.

Q: What is an *oikos*?

Legendary Greeks: Gaea

Representing the earth itself, Gaea was born of Chaos. The mother of all of the natural features of earth, Gaea was a supreme being honored by the Olympian gods as well as common Greeks. Gaea and Uranus (the starlit sky) produced the Titans, who were the first race on earth. Gaea was imagined by early Greeks to be a bountiful mother and is represented as a gigantic woman, to whom those Greeks offered gifts of fruit and grains.

Marriage

On the rare occasions that wealthy Athenian women were allowed to leave their homes, they were guarded by the men in the family. It would be a disgrace if an Athenian woman or girl met and fell in love with a non-Athenian. Marriage to a non-Athenian would mean that their children would not be citizens. Only citizens in Athens could own land or participate in government.

Getting married was not usually a matter of love in ancient Greece. It was a legal agreement. A young woman's father provided a **dowry**—money to pay for taking care of the bride—as part of the marriage agreement.

Divorce in Athens was acceptable. As you might expect, the laws favored men. To make it official, a man simply had to declare his intent to divorce in front of witnesses. A man nearly always retained custody of his children, though he was often required to return the dowry.

It was rarer for a woman to divorce her husband. Women were not allowed to bring cases to court, so a woman had to appeal to the city archons. Even if she was granted the divorce she was rarely allowed to keep her children.

words to know

terra-cotta: a hard, semi-fired, waterproof ceramic clay used in pottery and building construction.

dowry: the property that a woman brings to her husband at the time of the marriage.

barbarian: foreigners with an unnrecognizable language that sounded to the Greeks like "bar bar."

Children

Children in ancient Greece were kept under close watch, and bad behavior was dealt with harshly. Some fathers would even send a slave to school with their sons, to make certain that they didn't misbehave!

Still, children were allowed to play, just like kids today. You might even recognize some of the toys they played with: balls (*sphairai*), hoops, tops, dolls, yo-yos, and even miniature chariots. At age seven, young boys went to school. Young girls, on the other hand, were trained by their mothers at home in weaving and other household skills. Teachers in ancient Greece were called *grammatistes*.

Athenian Toddlers

Just like toddlers today, Athenian toddlers had to learn proper hygiene. Archaeologists discovered an ancient potty chair made of clay when they excavated an Athenian marketplace during the 1950s.

Slavery in Ancient Greece

The ancient Greeks kept slaves (or "helots") as early as 800 BCE, though no one knows the exact origins of this custom. Around 400 BCE historians believe that slaves made up about one-third of the Athenian population. People became slaves for different reasons. Some were kidnapped and sold into slavery, some were prisoners of war, and others were born into slavery.

Unlike slaves in early America, ancient Greek slaves were racially diverse. They came from many regions, including Thrace, Syria, and Lydia, and their status could vary. Domestic slaves worked in the home, grinding grain, washing clothes, and cleaning.

Houses at Olynthos

Olynthos was a town across the Aegean Sea from Athens in northeastern Greece. In the fourth century BCE King Philip of Macedon, father to Alexander the Great, wished to expand his empire into Olynthos. When Olynthians tried to resist King Philip's expansion, Philip ordered that the city be demolished. Because nothing was ever rebuilt there, the remains are a perfect opportunity for archaeologists to study how people lived at Olynthos.

Floor mosaic.

Archaeologists have excavated about 100 houses, finding things like brass door knockers, clay sculptures, and a bronze arrowhead.

The houses at Olynthos were made of sun-baked mud and laid out in a grid pattern with streets running between them. Some of the floors were decorated with mosaics—different colored pebbles arranged in a pattern and set into the mud floor.

Like most ancient Greek homes, these houses were built around courtyards situated to take advantage of temperature variations between seasons. A sheltered balcony along three sides of the courtyard faced south, allowing sunlight to reach into the courtyard to warm the residents during the cold, sometimes snowy winters. In the hot summer months, people could stay cool in the shade below the balconies. Archaeologists believe that these private courtyards were used for drying laundry as well as other day-to-day chores.

Athenian slaves were protected by law from physical abuse, but since slaves could not represent themselves in court, they seldom made official complaints. Starvation and flogging were two methods used to keep some slaves in line, but in many households slaves were treated kindly. These slaves were considered a part of the family and underwent a special initiation ceremony upon becoming a member of a household. The purpose of the ceremony was to invoke the protection of Hestia, goddess of the hearth.

Some slaves lived separately from their masters and acted as bankers, shop managers, ship's captains, and artisans. They were paid for their work and were required to give a portion of their income to their owners.

Slaves who earned a wage were sometimes offered the right to buy their freedom, thus becoming "freedmen."

Other slaves were owned by the city-state. Some worked alongside citizens on construction crews, building roads and public buildings. Others worked as jury clerks or coin testers. By far the most brutal situation for slaves was working in the silver mines in Laurium, a city in southeast Attica. Work in the mines continued 24 hours a day, with each slave doing a 10-hour shift. Most of the slaves were foreigners, called **barbarians**, who had been captured by pirates or soldiers. The slaves who worked the mines led a harsh life and faced exposure to lead, which was mixed with the silver. This caused many to die at an early age.

Q: Where does the word **barbarian** come from?

Helots in Sparta outnumbered the Spartans 10 to 1, meaning there were 10 slaves for every Spartan. They were treated harshly in order to prevent an uprising. They had no political rights and could be executed without a trial. They were considered the property of the state and were forced to work the land in exchange for a small portion of the harvest. Spartans felt that by keeping slaves fearful, they could keep slaves obedient.

Pasion, the Slave

Some Athenians refused to work at menial jobs, but these jobs still needed to be done. This provided opportunities for a limited number of slaves. One famous Athenian slave, named Pasion, began his service working at a bank. During a time of financial crisis in Athens, he generously gave money to the state. Because of his actions, he was eventually granted citizenship. When he died in 370 BCE, he was the richest banker and manufacturer in Athens.

activity: **Baklava**

Baklava is a rich pastry that may have originated in Asia Minor, then spread throughout the ancient Greek world during the archaic period.

INGREDIENTS

4	cups walnuts	20	sheets phyllo dough
1	tablespoon ground cinnamon	1½	cups sugar
¼	teaspoon ground cloves	1½	cups water
¾	cup sugar	1	teaspoon vanilla extract
2	sticks butter, melted	½	cup honey

1 Preheat oven to 350 degrees Fahrenheit. Finely chop the nuts and toss with cinnamon, cloves, and sugar. Set aside.

2 Unroll the phyllo dough and cover it with a dampened cloth to keep it from drying out as you work. Brush the bottom and sides of a 9-by-13-inch pan with melted butter. Place one sheet phyllo in the pan and brush completely with butter. Place another sheet on top and brush with butter. Repeat until you have 7 sheets layered, each brushed with melted butter.

3 Sprinkle one-third of the nut mixture on top, then layer three sheets of phyllo, each brushed with melted butter. Then in the same way, layer one-third of the nut mixture, three sheets of phyllo, final third of nut mixture, and seven sheets of phyllo.

4 Using a sharp knife cut diamond or triangle shapes into your baklava all the way to the bottom of the pan. Bake for about 30 minutes.

5 While your baklava is baking, bring the sugar, water, vanilla, and honey to a boil, then simmer for about 20 minutes.

6 Remove baklava from the oven and immediately spoon your sugar syrup over it. Let cool, recut your baklava, and enjoy!

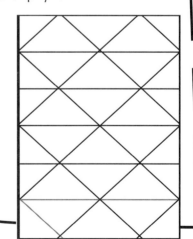

The Arts
of the Ancient Greeks

3

ANCIENT GREECE WAS A CULTURAL WONDERLAND, with art abundant in many forms. Storytellers performed epic poems, dramas, and comedies before large audiences. Architects designed grand buildings. Artists created pottery and sculpture that was both beautiful and useful. Ancient librarians collected handwritten copies of books from around the world.

The art of the ancient Greeks still influences us today. For example, many of our grand buildings look quite like some of the famous buildings of ancient Greece. Ancient Greek poets inspired Roman poets, who in turn influenced English poetry. The tradition of an orchestra to back up a stage performance is still practiced today. Students of literature still study the works of ancient Greek playwrights just as artists consider the statues and architecture of ancient Greece to be examples of some of the best in the world.

Oddly, though, as much as they liked to surround themselves with works of beauty, the ancient Greeks didn't always consider these things "art," as we do today. Their beautifully painted pottery, for example, was made to be useful. Greek sculptures were often used as public memorials, offerings, or markers for graves. But with these creations, the ancient Greeks left a legacy for the modern world.

Greek Literature and Drama

Literature fills our libraries and homes in the form of books. In the early days of ancient Greece, literature wasn't preserved in books, but was shared through storytelling. Poets performed tales, often accompanied by the music of a **lyre**, before audiences in a tradition known as ***rhapsodoi***. City-states across ancient Greece regularly held festivals where storytellers, also called *rhapsodoi*, competed for prizes. The popularity of *rhapsodoi* led to a new style of presentation that began around 486 BCE: **drama**.

The Muses

The ancient Greeks believed that nine goddesses, called muses, presided over the arts and sciences. The muses were daughters of the Greek god Zeus, and each was in charge of a different type of art. Poets, philosophers, and musicians all turned to their muses for guidance and inspiration. Take a look at the muses below, and you'll see how important poetry was to the ancient Greeks!

Calliope (kuh-li'-up-ee): the muse of epic poetry

Clio (kly'-oh): the muse of history

Euterpe (you-terp'-ee): the muse of lyric poetry (sung to flute music)

Melpomene (mel-pom'-un-ee): the muse of tragedy

Terpsichore (terp-sik'-or-ee): the muse of choral songs and the dance

Erato (air'-uh-toe): the muse of love poetry (sung to lyre music)

Polyhymnia (pol'-ee-him'-nee-uh): the muse of sacred poetry

Urania (you-ray'-nee-uh): the muse of astronomy

Thalia (the-lie'-uh): the muse of comedy

words to know

lyre: stringed instrument.

rhapsodoi: poetry performed as a story, often to music.

drama: Greek word meaning "action."

tragedy: a play that usually depicts events from a mythical past and that often ends sadly.

comedy: a play that makes the audience laugh by poking fun at politicians, famous people, and even the gods.

chorus: singers, dancers, and musicians who acted out the drama, told by a storyteller.

orchestra: the stage area used by the chorus.

Drama included performances of **tragedies**, which often told stories of the mythical past, and **comedies**, in which performers poked fun at politicians, famous people, and even the gods. This teasing was acceptable and audiences loved it. The earliest dramas were stories told by one storyteller backed up by a **chorus**. The Greek chorus was a group of singers, dancers, and musicians who acted out the drama of the story being told by the storyteller. The Greek chorus provided the appropriate background for the stories, transforming a simple spoken performance into a show to be admired. Their wailing demonstrated grief. Their songs rejoiced at triumph.

Q: What does **drama** mean in Greek? Hint: "lights, camera, _____!"

Over time, performances grew more complex, with lots of characters, although only three actors were allowed to perform at once. In order to portray a large cast of characters, the performers used many masks in each performance, changing them as they slipped into a different character. Masks were sometimes very elaborate, even frightening. Female characters were played by men wearing masks, because women were not allowed to perform.

Statue with a lyre.

Performances were often part of dramatic competitions. A panel of 10 *kritai*, or judges, wrote down their favorite performance on tablets, then placed them in an urn.

Five tablets were drawn from the urn and the performance with the most votes won. The act of choosing only five of the ten tablets allowed part of the decision to be made by the gods.

If an audience disliked the performance, they expressed it by throwing food and rocks at the performer.

The city of Athens held dramatic competitions in honor of the fertility god Dionysus in the grand Theatre of Dionysus. This theater held 14,000 people and was famous throughout ancient Greece. It was not the only theater. Many theaters were similar to the Theatre of Dionysus, though perhaps not as grand. They were circular, open-air buildings with seating that surrounded a round stage area called an orchestra. The orchestra wasn't a group of musicians as we think of it today, but was the part of the stage where the chorus performed.

These dramatic presentations were so popular that they inspired some ancient Greeks to write down the tales that were told. Some historians believe that Homer's *Iliad* and *Odyssey* were the first written stories in ancient Greece. It was the very first time people used the written word for recording history, and made the ancient Greeks interested in recording other things as well.

Recreation of the Theatre of Dionysus.

Spreading Knowledge with the Written Word

Spoken language existed long before the written word, and it was common for ancient Greeks to rely on memory alone when performing their *rhapsodoi*. But during the early part of the eighth century BCE, the Greeks met the Phoenicians, seafaring people from the coast of Syria. The ancient Greeks adapted the Phoenician alphabet and then used it to record Greek stories and history. Over the centuries, Greeks advanced from carving script onto clay tablets to writing on papyrus scrolls.

From 323 to 285 BCE, King Ptolemy I was the ruler of Egypt and Lydia, two Greek colonies on the Mediterranean Sea. The capital city of Egypt was Alexandria, a great seaport situated in the northern part of Egypt on the Mediterranean Sea. Alexandria was home to 300,000 free citizens plus many slaves and foreigners. It was the center of science, literature, and art in the Hellenistic world during Ptolemy's rule. In 288 BCE, Ptolemy established the grand Library of Alexandria, which was eventually filled with an estimated 500,000 scrolls of the best works from all over the world.

Lyre.

Greek Playwrights

Aristophanes was famous for writing comedies such as *The Clouds* and *The Birds* for two Athenian festivals, the Dionysia and the Lenea. He wrote at least 30 plays, but only 11 have survived. *Lysistrata*, Aristophanes's anti-war comedy, was translated into a book and illustrated many centuries later by the artist, Pablo Picasso.

Sophocles was a general in the Peloponnesian War, as well as a priest and a playwright. He is famous for the tragedies known as the three Theban plays: *Oedipus the King*, *Oedipus at Colonus*, and *Antigone*.

Historians believe that **Euripides** wrote more than 90 tragedies, 18 of which have survived. He broke Greek custom and included strong female characters and smart slaves in his stories.

Aeschylus was the first Greek playwright to introduce a second actor and dialogue (conversation) to his plays, and he made the chorus part of the dramatic action. Of the more than 90 plays he is believed to have written, only seven survive.

Know Your Ancient Greeks: Homer

Partly because of a man named Homer, literature became an important part of life in ancient Greece. Around 800 BCE, Homer created two stories, called *The Iliad* and *The Odyssey*. Written about the Trojan War and Odysseus's journey home after the war, the stories incorporated historical figures from the Mycenean age and many Greek gods and goddesses. These stories were told in verse and were quite long. Passed from generation to generation, children memorized the stories by singing the verses.

The Iliad and *The Odyssey* are two of the most famous stories from the ancient world. They were performed on stages throughout ancient Greece, and are even required reading for literature students today. Yet little is known about the author.

Historians believe that these epic poems were composed at Greek settlements on the coast of Asia Minor. But who wrote them? While Homer is generally acknowledged as the creator of both *The Iliad* and *The Odyssey*, some historians question whether he deserves all the credit. Homer is believed to have been a skilled storyteller, or *rhapsodoi*, but it's possible he was not the sole creator of these stories. In the oral tradition of storytelling, *rhapsodoi* could embellish their stories to make them more exciting. Is it possible that these stories—well-known Greek legends—could have been told by many different *rhapsodoi*, with a different twist at each telling? Perhaps then, Homer used a little creative license, combining the stories of other *rhapsodoi* into the two epic stories he is credited with today.

Historians still argue about whether Homer's epics are purely fiction or historically accurate. As archaeologists examine ancient artifacts, the debate continues. To some, the discovery of what is believed to be the city of Troy (read more in chapter 10) confirms Homer's claim of a Trojan War. Others argue there is no proof that Homer's stories were anything other than pure entertainment.

Unfortunately, we might never know for sure.

Poetry, mathematical theories, and scientific studies filled the library with a vast amount of knowledge and ideas.

These ancient Greeks took advantage of the many visitors to their city to support the library. When foreign ships docked in Alexandria any books found on board were copied (by hand, not with a copy machine!) and added to the library's collection. Because of the constant coming and going of foreigners, the library had works in a variety of languages, but Greek was the most common.

Piece of a papyrus scroll.

Scholars from all over the world were invited to visit the Library of Alexandria. Visitors are thought to have copied some of the works to take back to their homelands, spreading the knowledge held at Alexandria throughout the civilized world. Some works have survived only because people copied them—the Library of Alexandria suffered numerous fires over the years, the result of battles waged in the area.

King Ptolemy I.

Early Greek Writing

In 1900, an archaeologist named Arthur Evans discovered ancient clay tablets on the island of Crete as well as on mainland Greece. Remember, that's where the Minoans and Mycenaeans lived before the Greek dark age. On those tablets were two different types of script. In 1952, one of the languages on these tablets was deciphered and given the name Linear B. The other type of script, called Linear A, is still undeciphered! This indicates that even before the dark age, the Greeks made complex recordings of their language, even though little of it has survived.

Clay tablet with Greek alphabet.

activity:
Comedy and Tragedy Masks

You've read that the ancient Greeks used masks during their performances to convey different emotions. Think about how different emotions can look—how would you portray happy? Or sad? Or angry? Choose two different emotions and create your own double-sided mask.

1 Sandwich the wooden paint stirrer between two sturdy paper plates and glue together.

2 Either cut out eye holes or simply draw them on. One side of your mask can be comic, the other, tragic.

3 To make a comical mask, use bright colors and whimsical decorations like glitter, pom-poms, beads, and pipe cleaners. For a tragic mask, use dark, somber colors such as black, gray, and dark purple.

4 Glue pipe cleaners or yarn for hair around the upper edge of the mask on both sides. As you're decorating, remember that anything that extends beyond the edge of the mask will be visible from both sides of the mask.

5 Now, try telling a simple story, using the mask to portray different emotions. If you do the project with a friend, you can each take on a different part.

supplies

- ☒ **wooden paint stirrer or ruler**
- ☒ **2 sturdy paper plates**
- ☒ **glue**
- ☒ **scissors**
- ☒ **markers, glitter, pom-poms, beads, pipe cleaners, yarn** (in bright, cheerful colors and dark, somber colors)

activity:**Write a Letter in Greek**

Using the chart, write a letter to a friend. Because the symbols are so different from the letters of the English alphabet, it's almost like writing in code. In some cases the sound of a word is more important than its English spelling. For instance, you'll notice that the Greek alphabet doesn't have an *F*. So if you want to write the word *fantastic*, you'll need to use Φ to begin the word.

Make sure that when you send your Greek letter you also include a copy of the chart, so that your message can be deciphered.

Capital	Lower Case	Greek	English
A	α	Alpha	a
B	β	Beta	b
Γ	γ	Gamma	g
Δ	δ	Delta	d
E	ε	Epsilon	e
Z	ζ	Zeta	z
H	η	Eta	h
Θ	ϑ	Theta	th
I	ι	Iota	i
K	κ	Kappa	k
Λ	λ	Lambda	l
M	μ	Mu	m
N	ν	Nu	n
Ξ	ξ	Xi	x
O	o	Omicron	o
Π	π	Pi	p
P	ρ	Rho	r
Σ	σ	Sigma	s
T	τ	Tau	t
Θ	θ	Upsilon	u
Φ	φ	Phi	ph
X	χ	Chi	ch
Ψ	ψ	Psi	ps
Ω	ω	Omega	o

Aesop and His Fables

Do you remember the story of the lion and the mouse? A lion threatens to kill a mouse that is annoying him. The mouse begs for his life, suggesting that perhaps one day, he can repay the favor. The lion finds this suggestion comical, but lets the mouse go free. Lo and behold, one day, the lion finds himself caught in a trap made of rope. Guess who comes along and gnaws through the rope to free the King of Beasts? The moral of the story is that little friends can become great friends.

This is just one story of many famous fables that were recorded by a man called Aesop. He is thought to have been a freed slave living during the sixth century BCE. Aesop's fables featured animals with human characteristics and voices.. Each story had a moral, or lesson. Using animal characters allowed Aesop to comment on politics or morality without getting in trouble. He could present a story with circumstances that might be recognizable to his listeners, but by using animals in the story rather than a real person, he could easily claim that it was nothing more than a story about a silly animal.

Fables featuring animals had long been part of the oral storytelling tradition, but Aesop wrote the stories down. Aesop's fables are perhaps the most recognizable collection of fables in the world.

Pottery

Some of the most well-preserved **relics** of ancient Greece are clay pots, vases, and urns that were decorated with very detailed and distinctive patterns. These **artifacts** give us the opportunity to see, firsthand, works that were made in ancient times. Many of the pieces are decorated with scenes from ancient Greece, and this has helped historians piece together information about life during this time period. Images of food preparation, children learning to walk, and battles give us a glimpse into the life of ancient Greeks.

Athens was famous for its pottery, which was exported all over the world. Athenian pottery often featured red figures on a black background or back figures on a red background. Making these fabulous vases and urns required a potter, who formed the clay into a certain shape, and a painter, who created artistic patterns, figures, or elaborate scenes. These beautiful clay vessels were used in daily life for carrying water, serving food and drink, storing food, and displaying fruit and flowers.

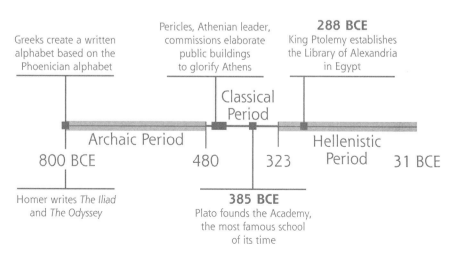

Two examples of Greek pottery.

words to know

relic: something that has survived from a long time ago.

artifact: an object made by a human, usually a tool or ornament, that has survived from a long time ago—an artifact is a kind of relic.

Sculpture

If you take a look at ancient Greek sculpture, one thing will be obvious: ancient Greeks were not embarrassed by nudity! Near the end of the archaic period, sculptors often honored the Greek god Apollo by creating works of nudes in the image of the *kouros*, or "youth." These statues were considered pleasing to look at, and sculptors felt that the beautiful Apollo would appreciate them. Greek sculptors were fascinated by the human form and worked to precisely replicate all of the details of an individual's body.

More often than not, sculptors in ancient Greece worked on commission—that is, someone hired them to create a particular work of art. For instance, a wealthy man might hire a sculptor to create a statue for his courtyard. Great sculptors were also hired to decorate the grand public buildings for the city-state.

Greeks create a written alphabet based on the Phoenician alphabet

Pericles, Athenian leader, commissions elaborate public buildings to glorify Athens

288 BCE
King Ptolemy establishes the Library of Alexandria in Egypt

Classical Period

Archaic Period

800 BCE

480

323

Hellenistic Period

31 BCE

Homer writes *The Iliad* and *The Odyssey*

385 BCE
Plato founds the Academy, the most famous school of its time

activity: Make a Pot

To form pots, the ancient Greeks used clay from the earth and fired it to make it strong. You can create a pot of your own—though it won't hold water—from air-dry clay. Either make your own clay or buy it from a craft store.

1 If you want to make your own clay, mix ½ cup cornstarch, ½ cup flour, and ½ cup salt. Slowly add warm water just until the mixture sticks together and can be shaped. If you'd like, you can add a little food coloring to the dough. Knead the dough until it is smooth. If you accidentally make it too sticky, just add a little more flour or cornstarch.

2 Using either your homemade dough or the store-bought clay, form a small pot. To make a pinch pot, start with a ball of clay and slowly pinch it into shape, forming a basin in the center and molding it into a circular shape.

supplies

- ☒ cornstarch, flour, salt, water, and food coloring OR
- ☒ store-bought air-dry clay
- ☒ waxed paper

Legendary Greeks: Medusa

Medusa was a beautiful maiden who caught the eye of the sea god Poseidon. Boldly, Poseidon charmed Medusa in the Temple of Athena. Enraged at this violation of her temple, Athena turned Medusa into a monster. Writhing snakes replaced the hair on her head and anyone who looked at her would immediately turn to stone.

Perseus, a Greek hero, was sent on a quest for the head of Medusa. He was befriended by the goddess Athena and the god Hermes, who gave him advice for his quest. Athena warned him not to look directly at Medusa and Hermes offered a sickle, a leather bag (to carry Medusa's head), and a pair of winged sandals that would carry him home. Accompanied by Athena, Perseus tracked down Medusa. Athena held her shiny shield so that Perseus could look into it as a mirror, rather than look directly at Medusa. Using this clever trick, Perseus cut off her head and carried it with him, using it to turn his enemies to stone. From Medusa's blood sprang Pegasus, the winged horse, and Chrysaor, a giant.

3 Another kind of pot to try is a coil pot. To make one, roll your clay into snake-like ropes that are about the thickness of a pencil. Make a circular base about ¼-inch thick, and start coiling it into a circle. When your coiled circle is about 3 inches across, start stacking the coils on top of each other, so that each time around your pot gets taller. If you'd like, you can use your fingers to smooth the inside of the pot.

Start to coil clay over base and keep it going in the shape you want your vase

4 Set your finished pot on waxed paper to air dry. Once it's dry, you can use your pot to hold small items on your desk or dresser.

Roll out handles and rough up the ends so they will adhere to the vase better

Once you have the shape you want, use water to smooth out the coils

Pericles, an Athenian leader during the classical period, felt that Athens should be worthy of admiration, so he commissioned elaborate public buildings with statues and **friezes**. The philosopher Plato, who in 385 BCE founded the Academy, the most famous school in the classical world, went so far as to suggest that the law only allow graceful buildings to be constructed!

Creating the sculptures that decorated ancient Greek buildings was a huge job. Temples were often decorated with larger-than-life marble statues and an ornamental band of carvings around the building called a frieze.

These sculptures and friezes might represent gods and goddesses, mythological stories, sporting activities, or historical events. Because statues on these buildings were so large, sculptors often set up shop near the construction site. That way, the finished statue had only a short distance to travel and, therefore, less risk of breaking.

Sculptors created a clay model of the statue before they began the final work in marble. Once the model was perfect, the **apprentices** would chisel the

Q: What is missing from the ancient **Greek statues** that still exist?

marble into its rough form. At this point, the master took over, chiseling the details and finishing touches with a sharp iron carving tool. The surface of the marble was usually smoothed with pumice, a type of rough stone.

With the carving complete, new craftspeople joined the project. They attached metal details, such as spears or harnesses, through holes the sculptor had drilled in appropriate places. Finally, painters applied wax and bright colors, until the statue seemed almost lifelike. The colors and wax have disappeared over the ages, so the grand Greek sculptures are more familiar to us in their plain white form.

Know Your Ancient Greeks: Phidias

Phidias was a famous sculptor born in Attica in the fifth century BCE. While none of his work is known to have survived, there is written documentation of it. Phidias was the general superintendent of public works in Athens. He supervised the building of the Parthenon as well as the Propylaea, the monumental entrance to the Acropolis (you'll read about these famous structures later). He was also hired to create a number of famous statues, including Athena

Statue of Zeus.

Parthenos and the statue of Zeus. Zeus was the father of the gods at Olympia, and this statue was considered Phidias's masterpiece.

Phidias was accused of stealing gold that was intended for the statue of Athena Parthenos. Some accounts have him dying in jail, while others say he was simply banished. A slightly different version says he was innocent of stealing the gold, but guilty of adding his portrait, as well as that of the Athenian ruler Pericles, to the shield of Athena. Whether these accusations were true or not, both ancient and modern critics agree that Phidias was indeed a great artist.

Bronze was another material used by ancient Greek sculptors. The earliest bronze statues were made by hammering sheets of metal into the appropriate shapes, then **riveting** them together. By the late archaic period, sculptors had developed a method they called lost wax casting. Sculptors first created a wax model, then covered it with clay. Then they heated this clay-covered sculpture, which caused the clay to harden and the wax to melt.

The sculptor poured the melted wax out of the clay mold, and poured in the **molten** metal. Once the metal hardened, the sculptor broke the clay mold to reveal a solid bronze reproduction of the original wax sculpture.

Pericles.

words to know

frieze: a carved band around a building.

apprentice: someone training for a profession.

bronze: a hard metal made from a mixture of copper and tin.

rivet: a short metal fastener.

molten: a liquid, created by melting with heat.

Bronze sculptures were finished with inset eyes of glass or stone, silver teeth and fingernails, and copper lips and nipples. These details combined to create an amazingly lifelike appearance.

Athena Parthenos

Athena was the goddess of wisdom, the practical arts, and warfare, and she was the protector of cities, especially Athens. A huge statue in the image of Athena was created by the famous sculptor Phidias to stand inside the Parthenon, a temple honoring Athena. You'll read more about the Parthenon later. The statue was made of ivory and gold, and featured images of a sphinx and griffins on her helmet. A sphinx was a creature with a lion's body and human head, and griffins were mythical creatures with a lion's body and an eagle's head. The head of Medusa was depicted on Athena's breast.

Athena held a figure of the goddess Victory in one hand and a spear in the other. The full-sized statue has not survived, but a few miniature copies give us an idea of just how grand this piece must have been.

4

Greek Gods

THE ANCIENT GREEKS WERE VERY RELIGIOUS PEOPLE. Religion wasn't confined to a certain day of the week or time of celebration, although the Greeks did have special religious holidays and festivals in honor of the gods. Rather, religious rituals were part of everyday life. Greeks always offered part of their meal to the gods. Public meetings, assemblies, and councils all began with a prayer. Before troops went off to battle, their general **sacrificed** one or more animals in honor of the gods to bring success to his troops.

You may recognize some of the Greek gods from Greek mythology. Our word *myth* comes from the Greek word *mythos*. To us, a myth is something that has no basis in fact. To ancient Greeks, a myth was a wonderful story that told about a fundamental truth—whether about the Greek gods or heroes, the natural world, or Greek society.

The beginnings of Greek religion are difficult to trace—but by about 900 BCE, the people of ancient Greece were **worshipping** the **pantheon** of gods that we still recognize today. While this pantheon of gods was known throughout the lands of ancient Greece, each *polis* also had a patron god. This was a special **deity**

Zeus on his throne atop Mount Olympus.

The ancient Greeks believed that the entrance to the home of the gods on Mount Olympus was through a gate of clouds. They thought the gods feasted on nectar and ambrosia and meddled in the lives of ancient Greeks living below.

Religious Holidays

Athens observed about 70 religious holidays each year. Many of these holidays were related to farming. The Eleusinian Mysteries was a holiday that honored Demeter, goddess of the harvest. This celebration lasted for 21 days. Athenian religious holidays were seen not only as a time to honor the gods, but also as a time of rest, since the Athenians didn't have a weekly day off.

that protected the *polis* and its people. Athena, for instance, was the patron goddess of Athens. Athenians worshipped Athena at special festivals, which included the **Panathenaea**. This celebration was held every four years and was the most important festival: it lasted for six days, and featured banquets, athletic contests, dancing, and music.

Mount Olympus

Mount Olympus is the highest peak in Greece and the ancient Greeks believed that it was the home of the major Greek gods. How could they believe that gods and goddesses lived in a place that was a part of this world? Probably because Mount Olympus, with its steep terrain, was largely inaccessible. Those who did try to climb the mountain discovered that the thin air up high made breathing difficult. This could easily have been interpreted to mean that the mountaintop wasn't meant for **mortals**.

words to know

sacrifice: to offer something of value to a god.

worship: to show great devotion and respect, to pray.

pantheon: a group of gods, heroes, or important people all considered collectively.

deity: form of god or higher being.

Panathenaea: an Athenian festival held in mid-August celebrating Athena's birthday.

mortal: someone who can die—the opposite of immortal, like gods, who cannot die.

The Greek gods differ from the gods of other cultures in that they are famous for their interference in the lives of ancient Greek mortals. The gods argued among themselves and often used the people of Greece in their attempts to "best" another god. They often behaved badly just like humans, acting petty, jealous, and angry. As the stories go, the gods even moved from Mount Olympus to the real world to flirt with mortals or cause trouble.

The summit of Mount Olympus.

Greek Temples

The grand temples of ancient Greece were built more to honor the gods than for use by citizens. People did not come together for services or prayer at a temple, the way people worship at a church or temple today. Rather, the citizens of ancient *poleis* visited their temples whenever they wanted, to offer a sacrifice to the temple's god or to pray. A temple in ancient Greece was seen as the earthly home of a god, and the Greeks believed that the god visited and spent time in the temple.

Legendary Greeks: King Midas

According to legend, Midas was made king of Phrygia by the will of the gods, but he began his life as a peasant boy. He was convinced that money was all-important, so when the god Dionysus granted him one wish, King Midas asked that everything he touched be turned to gold. For a while, King Midas reveled in his golden touch. He had to rethink the idea, though, when he became hungry—as he began to eat his meal, it turned to gold. He called for his wine, but it, too, turned to gold.

King Midas begged Dionysus to help him be rid of this curse. Dionysus instructed King Midas to wash himself in the River Pactolus to remove the golden spell. Since that day, the banks of the river have been flecked with gold.

Temples were also filled with wealth and acted as a kind of storehouse for each *polis*. Money and valuables were sometimes left at the temple as gifts to the god, while other people used it as a place to store their own valuable items—surely nobody would dare steal valuables from such a **sacred** place!

Worship

The worship of ancient Greek gods was part of daily life. People worshipped the gods publicly at altars placed outside of temples, or privately at the **altars** common in most ancient Greek households.

The two most important aspects of worship were prayer and sacrifice. Greek worshippers prayed in a standing position, hands raised to the heavens. Kneeling and touching the ground was to call on the gods from below, called the underworld.

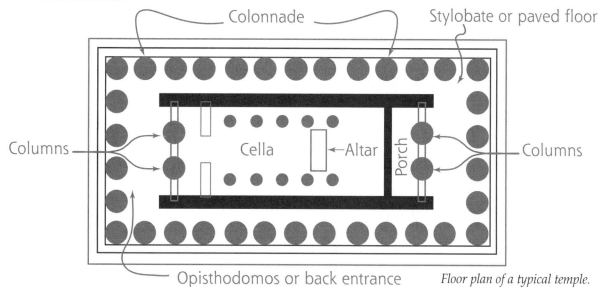

Floor plan of a typical temple.

Greeks making a sacrifice to the gods on an altar.

The simplest sacrifice made to please a god involved leaving food or wine at an altar. During some rituals, people sacrificed animals. When the Greeks sacrificed an animal it was with much ceremony. The animal was draped with flowers and sprinkled with barley to make it lower its head. This was seen as submission to its killing. The altar was **purified** with water.

The animal was killed and its blood was drained into a bowl and sprinkled on the altar or over the worshippers. The animal was then cooked and eaten by the worshippers. An animal sacrifice was seen not only as a sacred **ritual**, but as a rare opportunity to eat meat.

While it is common for us to celebrate funerals and weddings in churches or temples, the ancient Greeks did not do this. The head of the household led private ceremonies. At large public ceremonies, the head of state officiated.

Oracles

Oracles were usually peasant women who passed messages between gods and humans. People would seek advice from the gods by asking the oracle a question. The answer was usually vague, with many possible **interpretations**.

words to know

sacred: something very special, worthy of worship.

altar: a raised table or structure where religious ceremonies take place.

purify: to clean, make something pure.

ritual: a set of formal actions that is repeated in a ceremony.

oracle: a source of wisdom or knowledge.

interpretation: an explanation of the meaning or importance of something.

trance: in a dazed or hypnotized state, unaware of the surroundings.

prophet: someone who claims to be the voice of god, or who predicts the future.

prophecy: a prediction of a future event.

Know Your Ancient Greeks: Heracles

Heracles (sometimes called Hercules) was the son of Zeus and Alcmene, a mortal woman. When Heracles was a baby, his jealous stepmother, Hera, tried to kill him by placing a serpent in his cradle. But Heracles was a baby with super-human strength, and the baby Heracles killed the serpent. Hera's jealous ways finally drove Heracles insane, and he killed his own wife and children. Shamed by his insanity, Heracles asked an oracle how to regain his honor. He was instructed to serve Eurystheus, king of Mycenae, for 12 years. The king wasn't sure what tasks to set for the mighty Heracles, so he consulted Hera. They came up with 12 tasks for Heracles.

Known as the 12 labors of Heracles, these tasks included such feats as killing the nine-headed hydra, who would sprout two new heads for every wound. Heracles also had to bring Cerberus, the three-headed dog of Hades, from the underworld.

Heracles completed his tasks and was finally free to return to Thebes, where he married Deianira. Upon his death, Heracles was taken to Mount Olympus and became immortal.

Many temples in ancient Greece had oracles. The most famous of them was the Temple of Apollo at Delphi in central Greece. The three oracles at Delphi were all over the age of 50, which was considered quite old at the time.

When an oracle was called upon, she first purified herself in a sacred spring. Then she drank water from a different spring near the temple. Seated on a three-legged stool that was positioned over a crack in the rock floor, the oracle went into a trancelike state. She may have chewed or inhaled the smoke of bay leaves or taken drugs to to go into the **trance**. Some historians think that the crack in the rock gave off a kind of gas that induced a trancelike state.

In this state, the oracle uttered words that seemed to come directly from the gods. A male **prophet** would interpret the oracle's **prophecy**, sometimes in a verse that left more questions than answers.

Q: **Where** did the ancient Greeks believe **the gods** lived and visited?

Most of the questions people asked the oracles were of a personal nature, though on occasion, a statesman might come for guidance in creating laws or going to war.

In ancient times, Delphi was considered to be the center of the world because of the presence of the oracle at the Temple of Apollo.

In 480 BCE, with the Persians invading mainland Greece, Athenian leaders consulted the oracle at Delphi. They were told their only hope was the defense provided by a "wooden wall." Some people thought that they should build walls of wood around Athens, but their leader, Themistocles, guessed that the oracle was referring to a fleet of wooden ships.

With the Greek navy, he lured the Persians into a narrow area between the island of Salamis and the port of Piraeus. Despite being outnumbered, the Greeks crushed the Persians in the Battle of Salamis, the first great naval battle in recorded history.

The Gods Walk Among Us

Ancient Greek culture had dozens of gods and godlike creatures. The major gods who resided on Mount Olympus were a crucial part of ancient Greek culture. Other divine beings were called demigods. They were half mortal, half god, and were born of unions between the gods and humans. Some of the demigods are Heracles (Hercules), Alexander the Great, and Achilles.

Selling Shoes with Greek Gods

Nike is the Greek goddess who symbolized triumph and victory. The ancient Greeks counted on her to preside over both athletic and military contests. Nike is one of the few goddesses who is depicted with wings. Can you imagine why a shoe company might want to use her name?

The Nike of Samothrace.

52

The important Greek gods are:

- Gaea, the earth goddess, married to Uranus.
- Uranus, the sky god, had many children with Gaea, including the 12 Titans.
- Cronos, the leader of the Titans, gained power by defeating his father, Uranus. Cronos worried that his children would take power away from him, so he ate his children to protect his position—all of his children, that is, except for Zeus, who was saved from this fate by his fast-thinking mother, Rhea.
- Aphrodite, the goddess of love and beauty.
- Apollo, the sun god, also god of music, light, and truth. Each day, Apollo drove a chariot that pulled the sun across the sky.
- Ares, the god of war.
- Artemis, goddess of the hunt and the moon, twin sister of Apollo.
- Athena, goddess of wisdom, cities, handicrafts, and agriculture. She sprang from Zeus's forehead fully grown, so she didn't have a mother.
- Demeter, goddess of the harvest.
- Hades, the lord of the underworld and the god of wealth, due to all the precious metals that come from underground.

Cronos.

- Hephaestus, god of fire and metalworking.
- Hera, wife of Zeus, the protector of women and marriage.
- Hermes, the god of thieves and commerce. He was the fastest of the gods and responsible for guiding the dead to the underworld.
- Hestia, goddess of the hearth.
- Nike, the goddess of victory.
- Poseidon, the god of the sea. He was extremely important to the Greeks since they traveled across the Aegean Sea all the time.
- Zeus, god of the earth and heavens, and the rain. He became the leader of the Olympians after he defeated his father, Cronos, and banished the Titans.

Zeus.

Unlike Christianity, which has the Bible, and Islam, which has the Koran, Greek religion had no single text that believers could read and follow. Young Greeks learned about the gods by listening to stories, and when they grew up, they told the same stories to their children. These myths about the gods described how they were born, and about their special powers, love affairs, and rivalries.

Legendary Greeks: Zeus

Zeus was the sixth son of Rhea and the Titan Cronus. It was prophesied that Cronus would be overthrown by one of his children. To prevent this, Cronus swallowed every child born to him. Rhea, expecting her sixth child, fled to Crete and gave birth to Zeus. Afterward, she wrapped a stone to look like a baby and tricked Cronus into swallowing the stone, rather than Zeus. Later, Zeus and his cousin Metis conspired to give Cronus a drug that made him throw up Zeus's siblings.

Zeus and his brothers, Poseidon and Hades, drew straws to divide the world between them. Zeus became the supreme ruler of the heavens, Poseidon ruled the sea, and the underworld was ruled by Hades. Along with many of the other major Greek gods, Zeus resided on Mount Olympus.

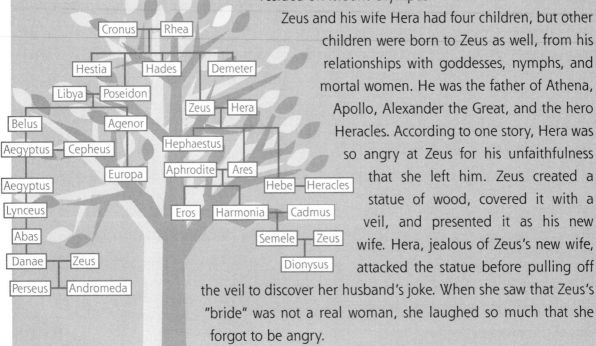

Zeus and his wife Hera had four children, but other children were born to Zeus as well, from his relationships with goddesses, nymphs, and mortal women. He was the father of Athena, Apollo, Alexander the Great, and the hero Heracles. According to one story, Hera was so angry at Zeus for his unfaithfulness that she left him. Zeus created a statue of wood, covered it with a veil, and presented it as his new wife. Hera, jealous of Zeus's new wife, attacked the statue before pulling off the veil to discover her husband's joke. When she saw that Zeus's "bride" was not a real woman, she laughed so much that she forgot to be angry.

activity: **Supreme Sales**

Just as Nike uses the name of a Greek goddess for a product, other companies use names that you'll recognize from ancient Greek mythology as well. Think about Midas mufflers, Olympus cameras, Amazon.com, and Ajax cleanser! Midas was a king who could turn all that he touched into gold. Ajax was a hero of the Trojan War and the Amazons were a race of women warriors in Greek mythology. How would you use the Greek gods and goddesses, and other ancient heros, to market a product?

HERACLES GYM

BRING OUT THE GREEK GOD IN YOU!

Bring this ad in when you join and receive a 10% discount.

100 Main Street
Anytown, USA

555-1234

1 Think about the attributes of some of your favorite gods and heroes of ancient Greece. Heracles for instance, was strong—he'd be a great representative for a gym.

2 Come up with a product that is well suited to the god you choose. You can either use a product that is already available to consumers, or develop one of your own.

3 Think about how your god relates to the product and how he or she could be used to convince people that your product is the one to buy.

4 On poster board, create an advertisement. Include a slogan (a short saying about your product), an image of the product, and a picture of the god or goddess you're using in your ad campaign. Add any other information you think will help sell your product.

5 You can even take it further and write a 30-second TV or radio advertisement.

supplies

- ☒ **poster board**
- ☒ **markers**

activity: Creature Feature

Some of the demigods and famous creatures from the stories of ancient Greece were combinations of man and beast, or otherwise different from human form. Medusa, with snakes for hair, was one. Others were Pegasus, the winged horse who sprang from the blood of Medusa when she was slain by Perseus, and Chiron the centaur, with a human head and torso on a horse's body. Triton was a merman, son of Poseidon and his mortal wife. Human down to his waist, Triton had the tail of a fish instead of legs. When gods and humans joined in creating offspring, anything could happen!

You can create your own album of creatures that change with the turn of a page.

1 Use a 3-hole punch to punch holes along one 11-inch side of all 10 sheets of cardstock.

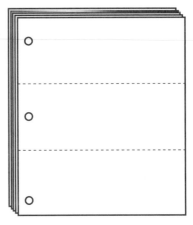

supplies

- ☒ **ten 8½-by-11-inch sheets of white cardstock**
- ☒ **3-hole punch**
- ☒ **ruler**
- ☒ **pencil**
- ☒ **scissors**
- ☒ **markers**
- ☒ **small binder**

2 Use the ruler and pencil to divide the sheets into three equal sections. Each section should have one punched hole.

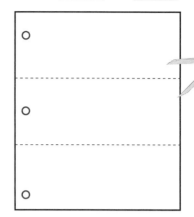

3 Cut along these lines, making sure to keep the top, middle and bottom sections together. Put the sections into the binder. You have a section for the head, torso, and legs of 10 creatures.

4 Before you begin drawing your creatures, you need to mark the paper so that all these parts will line up correctly. Make small marks about two inches apart at the same place on every piece of cardstock where the pieces meet. You can do this by first marking the top pieces, then, one at a time, flip the top and bottom sections out of the way and draw matching marks on each new section. Then flip the middle section and mark the next one to match the top and bottom marks.

5 Now you can draw different creatures. Just make certain that you draw a head on the upper section, a torso on the middle section, and legs and feet on the bottom, and that the body parts are aligned with the marks you made where the paper meets.

6 Once you've drawn all of your creatures, you can flip the pages in sections to create all kinds of unusual combinations.

5 Sports and the Olympics

SPORTS ARE A BIG PART OF AMERICAN CULTURE. FOR MANY kids, the weekend revolves around soccer, baseball, or basketball. Professional sports are available to watch on TV at just about any time of day. Even people who aren't particularly interested in sporting events get caught up in the Olympic Games.

The Olympic Games that capture our attention every two years got their start in ancient Greece in 776 BCE. While other ancient cultures had sporting events of their own, no event has proved as influential, as important, or as longstanding as the Olympics.

The Olympic Games get their name from the village in which they were held: Olympia, which is located about 300 miles southwest of Mount Olympus. The games were part of a religious and cultural festival to honor Zeus, the father of the Greek gods, and were part of what is known as the **Panhellenic Cycle**.

The Panhellenic Cycle was a series of four festivals that combined celebrations to honor a particular god with athletic competition. The other Panhellenic festivals held in ancient Greece included the Nemean Games held

Panhellenic Cycle

The Panhellenic Cycle events were considered the most important athletic competitions of ancient Greece. The Olympiad was the four-year schedule for the different festivals: the Olympic Games were held in year one; the Nemean and Isthmian games were held in different months of year two; the Pythian Games were held in year three; and the Nemean and Isthmian games were held again in different months of year four. The cycle then started again with the Olympic Games. Individual athletes could participate in all of the games, and if an athlete won at all four he was especially honored as a ***periodonikes***, which means "circuit winner."

in Nemea, (also to honor Zeus), the Isthmian Games near Corinth (to honor Poseidon, the god of the sea), and the Pythian Games at Delphi (to honor Apollo, the god of light).

What made these four festivals different from local festivals that featured athletic events was that the Panhellenic Cycle events invited all free-born Greeks from throughout ancient Greece and the Greek colonies to compete. Athletes traveled from as far away as modern-day Spain and Turkey to compete in the different Panhellenic Games.

The Olympic Games were held during the summer and were arranged so that a full moon lit the celebrations on the third night.

Before and during the Olympic Games, an ***ekecheiria***, or truce, was announced, so that athletes and religious worshippers could travel safely to and from Olympia. While the truce was in effect, legal disputes were forbidden, wars were suspended, and armies were not allowed to enter Elis, the city-state where Olympia was located.

words to know

Panhellenic: all Greek.

Panhellenic Cycle: a series of four religious and cultural festivals.

ekecheiria: the Greek word for truce, literally means "holding of hands."

periodonikes: the Greek work for circuit winner. From the words *peri* and *hodos*, meaning "going around in a circle," and Nike, the goddess of victory who presided over all athletic and military contests.

Winning Panhellenic athletes were awarded a crown of wild olive leaves at Olympia, a crown of wild celery at Nemea and Corinth, and a crown of laurel leaves at Delphi. The honor of winning events in these festivals was so great that when they returned home, athletes were often showered with glory and gifts, such as leadership roles in the community or free meals for the rest of their lives.

In the early Olympics, judges didn't necessarily divide the men and boys into separate age groups, but rather divided them by physical size and strength.

And They're Off!

For at least the first 50 years, the only event at the Olympic Games was the **stadion**, a footrace roughly 200 meters long, which was the length of the stadium. This distance was called a **stade**.

In 724 BCE, a second race was added, called the **diaulos**, or double-stade.

The Stadium.

Diaulos runners ran the length of the track, made a sharp turn around a post, and returned back down the track. This new event was likely popular because at the next Olympics in 720 BCE, another new race was introduced. The **dolichos**, as it was called, equaled 24 lengths of the stadium.

Runners started the races from a standing crouch. Stones were set into the ground at the starting line, and runners curled their toes into the dirt at the edge of the stones, a space called the **balbis**, so they could get a fast start. In today's Olympic races, a runner who makes a false start—that is, who runs before the starting gun is fired—gets one more chance to start the race correctly. Runners in ancient Greece had it much tougher. Racers who committed a false start, in addition to being disqualified, could be whipped!

Q: How many festivals were in the Panhellenic Cycle and in what order did they take place?

In later years, officials learned how to prevent false starts in a much less violent way. They planted posts in the ground at

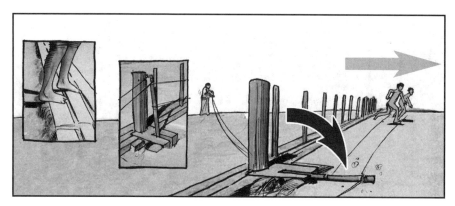

each end of the *balbis* and attached twisted ropes that pulled the posts to the ground. They then pulled the posts into a vertical position, placed a rope across the posts, and attached the rope to a trigger. This rope was chest-high on the athletes and kept them from making a false start.

At the start of the race, the official would hit a trigger, and the **hysplex**, as this device was known, would fall, dropping the rope to the ground and letting the runners sprint off.

words to know

stadion: a short footrace, roughly 200 meters long, named after the building it was held in.

stade: 200-meter distance.

diaulos: a footrace roughly 400 meters long.

dolichos: a footrace roughly 4,800 meters long.

balbis: the starting line.

hysplex: the starting gate that ensured all runners started at the same time in ancient Greek running races.

Games for the Guys—and a Few for the Girls

The Olympic Games were open to any free-born Greek in the world, and all athletes competed in the nude. By being naked, they could show off their physique and the result of all their hard training. The Greek word for naked is *gymnos*, and the word **gymnasium** originally meant a place to exercise in the nude.

As for women, not only couldn't they compete in the Olympics—some couldn't even watch. Unmarried girls were allowed to attend the games, but any married woman found in the stadium (other than the priestess of Demeter who oversaw the games) was supposed to be punished by being thrown off Mount Typaeum. Whether or not this ever actually happened isn't clear, since there doesn't seem to be any record of it.

One woman who did make it inside the stadium and lived to tell the tale was named Callipateira (although some accounts of the story give her name as Pherenice). Callipateira was a widow who cut her hair short and disguised herself as a male trainer so that she could watch her son, Peisirodus, compete in his event. When Peisirodus won, she ran out to congratulate him, but while doing so was exposed as a woman.

Because her dead husband, Diogoras, and another son had also been successful athletes, Callipateira wasn't punished—but at future events everyone in the stadium had to be naked, not just the athletes.

While women weren't allowed to compete directly in the Olympics, they were allowed to enter equestrian (horse riding) events as the owner of either chariots or single horses. In fact, the winner of the first chariot and horse race recorded at the Olympics was a woman named Belistiche.

Growth of the Games

As the years passed, more and more events were added to the Panhellenic Games: wrestling, boxing, chariot racing, the **pankration**, horse racing, and the **pentathlon**. The *pankration* was a combat event combining striking and wrestling, while the pentathlon was a series of five events including discus, long jump, running, javelin, and wrestling. Believe it or not, the philosopher Plato was also a wrestler and a two-time winner of the Olympic *pankration*!

One important thing to note about all of these events is that they were individual competitions. Working together to achieve an athletic goal was valued less than individual strength and stamina. So it was every man for himself.

Since they were excluded from the Olympics, women eventually started holding their own sporting events at a separate festival in Olympia to honor Hera, the wife of Zeus. Unlike the men, who competed naked, women wore tunics, a knee-length garment that revealed only one shoulder when they competed.

words to know

gymnasium: place to exercise in the nude.

pankration: unarmed combat combining hitting and wrestling with very few rules.

pentathlon: a series of five events including discus, long jump, running, javelin, and wrestling, from the words penta, meaning "five," and athlon, meaning "contest."

Marathon: the village where the Greeks won a major battle over the Persians, and a running race of 26 miles, 385 yards (42.195 kilometers).

The Spirit of the Games

High standards and an honest performance were expected from Olympic athletes. Any athlete found to have cheated was fined, and the money collected was spent on a bronze statue of Zeus that was placed on the road that led to the stadium.

The *Pankration*

The *pankration* was a combination of wrestling and boxing, and the only restrictions were against biting and gouging out an opponent's eyes, nose, or mouth with fingernails. Competitors fought each other until one man was either knocked out or admitted defeat. Some *pankration* competitors specialized in particularly brutal methods of winning, including breaking fingers or putting strangleholds on their opponents. And kicking in the belly? Perfectly legal.

A message describing the athlete's offense was placed on the statue so athletes would be warned not to cheat.

Despite the high standards, athletes did occasionally get a little tricky with the rules. One story tells of Sotades, an athlete from Crete who won the *dolichos* at the 99th games. When Sotades competed in the next games four years later, he declared himself an Ephesian, claiming he was from the city Ephesus in Asia Minor. Turns out that the Ephesian people had bribed Sotades to give them a chance at winning.

From Ancient to Modern

The Olympic Games were held every four years from 776 BCE until 393 CE—a period of more than 1,100 years. But by 393 CE, the Romans had taken control of ancient Greece, and the Roman emperor, Theodosius, outlawed the games and the "pagan cults" that sponsored them. The word *pagan* refers to the belief in multiple gods.

It took more than 1,500 years for the Olympic Games to be held again. In 1894, Frenchman Baron Pierre de Coubertin proposed a revival of the games to promote athletic competition and improve foreign relationships. He founded the International Olympic Committee. While he wanted to hold the Olympics in Paris in 1900, the response to his idea was so enthusiastic that the games were held just two years after they were proposed, in 1896, in Athens. In 2004, 108 years later, the summer Olympics were again held in Greece, and the shotput event was hosted in the Stadium of Ancient Olympia, site of the original Olympic Games.

The five intertwined rings of the modern Olympic flag represent the unity of the five continents. The white background symbolizes the field and the colors of the rings—red, blue, green, yellow, and black—were carefully chosen so that every nation had at least one of their flag colors represented.

ZEUS

DIMITRIUS CHEATED IN THE LONG JUMP

The Modern Ancient Greek Event

Most people think of the **marathon** as an event from ancient Greece, but the first marathon actually took place in 1896, when the modern Olympic Games began. Although the marathon itself is new, the idea for the marathon does come from an ancient Greek legend.

Marathon

General Miltiades led the Greeks to victory over the Persians in 490 BCE. The battle took place in the village of Marathon, northeast of Athens. As the story goes, Miltiades then ordered a runner to carry news of the triumph back to Athens. This runner, Pheidippides, ran approximately 25 miles from the city of Marathon to Athens, shouting "Rejoice, we conquer!" to all he passed in the city. Then he dropped dead.

Athens

This story may or may not be true, but in either case, it hasn't scared away modern marathon runners.

From the original Olympics, with its single event, the games have evolved to include both summer and winter games. In 1994 the schedule changed from every four years, to alternating summer and winter games every two years. The modern Olympics include some events from the original games, such as the discus throw and running races, but most are new. There are now 28 sports included, with many of the sports divided into numerous events; for instance, in gymnastics, there are individual competitions for balance beam, floor exercise, bars, and vault. Recent Olympic Games have hosted athletes from as many as 200 different nations.

activity: Hold Your Own Ancient Olympics—and Crown the Winners

This activity will give you an idea of what the first Olympic events were like. In the ancient Olympics, the only prizes for the winners were laurel wreaths. Unlike the ancient Olympians, you may not live where laurel grows—but you can still make wreaths for the winners of your Olympics.

1 First figure out just how many meters a *stadion*, *diaulos*, and *dolichos* event would cover. What modern Olympic events could these be comparable to? Next, go outside and measure a stade. Mark the courses.

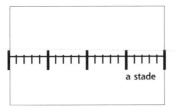

a stade

2 Take eight or nine long grass or flower stems and bunch them together, making the ends even. Fasten a rubber band or bag tie around one end to keep them from slipping. Carefully divide the stems into three sections, and braid them together. Or, you can divide the bunch of stems in half and twist them around each other, using a fastener or two partway. Secure the other end with the other rubber band, and fasten the two ends to form a wreath. Stick extra flowers or leaves into the braid for decoration and to cover up the fasteners.

3 Hold your events. Have a starting line and an official start: "On your mark, get set, go!" Time how long it takes to complete *stadion*, *diaulos*, and *dolichos* races.

4 In the ancient Olympics, laurel wreaths were worn on the back of the winner's head, tucked behind the ears. Crown your Olympic winners with your own version of an Olympic wreath.

supplies

- ☒ **tape measure**
- ☒ **8 or 9 stalks of long grass, or long-stemmed flowers** (carefully take off the flower heads, leaving a little bit of stem—you'll use these later)
- ☒ **2 or more small rubber bands or bag ties**
- ☒ **extra flower heads or leaves**
- ☒ **stopwatch**

6

Philosophy

THE WORD **PHILOSOPHY** MEANS "DEVOTION TO UNCOMMON knowledge" or "a man who likes to be wise." The ancient Greeks are famous for their advances in philosophy. Greek philosophers spent most of their lives pondering

WHY?

difficult questions. While many of their theories have been proven false over time, the fact that they were even asking these questions is important. It prompted the following generations to change the way they approached the unknown, to question common

WHERE?

reason, and to ask *Why?* Have you ever wondered why we are here? Or where things come from? Or what things are made up of?

Ancient Greek philosophers moved beyond pure acceptance of the world around them and asked such questions. They used reason and observation to answer their questions, and their findings affected science, math, and geography.

The question "What are things made of?" was one that was pondered by many different philosophers. Each

WHAT?

arrived at a different conclusion. Dirt and rocks are different from wood and water.

They look different and feel different. But many philosophers felt that everything in the universe had to have a common base.

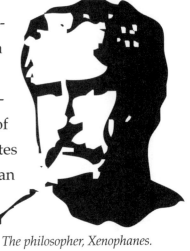

The philosopher, Xenophanes.

FATE

Greek philosophers searched for commonsense answers to questions. They developed logic and rules of argument that are still used in courts of law and debates today. They realized that for every view, there is often an opposing view. For instance, while rainy weather is good for the crops, it can also cause problems like leaky roofs or flooding.

Think about the big questions. How would you answer them? If you discuss these questions with a friend, there's a good chance that he or she may have a different opinion. You'll notice that it's difficult to separate these philosophical questions from religion or science. Different religious beliefs affect a person's answer to all of these questions. So how can there be any one answer to these questions?

RIGHT & WRONG

Even in ancient Greece, the questions asked by philosophers were tied up with religious beliefs. Xenophanes (560–478 BCE) was just one of many philosophers who doubted the stories told about the Greek gods and goddesses. He questioned the belief that immortals looked

The Big Philosophical Questions

Though philosophy had its start in ancient Greece, even today people ponder some tough philosophical questions.

- There are ethical questions: What is right? What is wrong? How do you know, and who decides?
- There are questions about the universe and its origins: How did the world come to be? Is there a system to the world? Did God create the world? How do you know?
- There are questions about our destiny: Can we tell the future? Are our lives planned out for us by fate, or do we choose our destiny?

Greek Saying

Have you ever heard the saying "you can't step into the same river twice?" Read this poem:

The river where you set your foot just now is gone—
those waters giving way to this, now this. *

This poem was written by Heraclitus, an early Greek philosopher who lived in the late sixth century BCE. He believed that all things are constantly in a state of flux, or change. Years later, both Plato and Aristotle dismissed him as being illogical.

A saying that we still use today has its roots in ancient Greece!

*(translated by Brooks Haxton in the New England Review, Winter 2001)

just like human beings. He wrote, "The Ethiopians say that their gods are black. If horses could draw, they would draw their gods looking like horses." Some philosophers even began to question whether the gods existed at all. But ordinary people still believed in the gods, and philosophers' questions made them nervous. It seemed dangerous to doubt the gods.

Socrates (469–399 BCE)

Socrates is one of the most famous ancient Greek philosophers, yet there is no record of his ever having written a word. Socrates didn't record what he discovered, or how he made his discoveries. He felt that knowledge was a living thing. Everything that we know about Socrates comes from the writings of others.

Socrates had an interesting idea about his own knowledge. While many ancient Greeks considered him to be a very smart man, he felt that there was so much to

DESTINY

ORIGIN OF THE UNIVERSE

know that, in reality, he knew nothing. He thought it was his understanding that he didn't know everything that made him knowledgeable.

Most Greek thinkers before Socrates had tried to answer the question "What is the world really like?" But Socrates cared only about studying how one should live—that is, how a person should interact with his or her fellow human beings. Instead of questioning the universe and everything in it, like other philosophers did, he might ask questions like "What is courage?" or "what is friendship?"

Socrates felt so strongly about his ideas that he even opposed the study of the natural world. He thought people would be better off if they searched for truth and learned how to deal honestly with one another. In his opinion, people should investigate which qualities or virtues lead one to live a good life, then define those virtues in such a way that others can follow the same path.

This concentration on morality and the best way to live led Socrates to develop a unique style of reasoning. To this day it is called the **Socratic method**, in his honor. To get at the heart of goodness, justice, and other virtues, Socrates asked questions of others, listened to their answers, and probed them for contradictions. If one answer proved false, Socrates would ask questions that led down a different path of reasoning in search of the true answer. Through this process of trial and error, Socrates and his listeners would eventually reach an answer that satisfied them all.

Q: How might religion answer philosophical questions?

words to know

philosophy: a quest for truth through logical reasoning, from the Greek word meaning lover of wisdom.

Socratic method: a way of finding the truth through a series of questions.

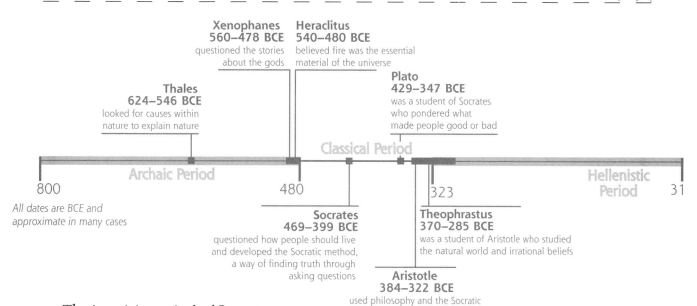

Xenophanes
560–478 BCE
questioned the stories
about the gods

Heraclitus
540–480 BCE
believed fire was the essential
material of the universe

Plato
429–347 BCE
was a student of Socrates
who pondered what
made people good or bad

Thales
624–546 BCE
looked for causes within
nature to explain nature

Classical Period

Archaic Period

Hellenistic
Period

800

480

323

31

All dates are BCE and
approximate in many cases

Socrates
469–399 BCE
questioned how people should live
and developed the Socratic method,
a way of finding truth through
asking questions

Theophrastus
370–285 BCE
was a student of Aristotle who studied
the natural world and irrational beliefs

Aristotle
384–322 BCE
used philosophy and the Socratic
method to study the natural world

The inquiring mind of Socrates eventually resulted in his death. His determination to question everything and everyone caused the leaders of ancient Greece to become angry. In his quest for knowledge, he was so bold as to question the existence of the gods, something that angered many Greeks—and probably scared them a bit, too. Socrates was accused of corrupting the youth of Athens. For this he was sentenced to death.

His friends wanted to help him escape from prison, but Socrates felt that it was important to comply with the law and die for his beliefs. Socrates, one of the greatest minds in ancient Greece, was forced to take his own life by drinking poison in the year 399 BCE, at the age of 70. One of Socrates's students, Plato, continued his work.

Plato (429–347 BCE)

Plato was born in Athens to a very wealthy family. When Plato was young, he listened to and learned from the great philosopher Socrates. Plato had great respect for Socrates and was very upset when he died. Plato wrote down some of the things he had heard Socrates speak about, which is how we know about Socrates today.

Q: Who did **Plato** believe should be **running** the **government**?

Soon, Plato began writing down some of his own ideas. He wrote about government, politics, and the natural world. In Plato's opinion, a few great people should make all of the decisions in government, because he didn't think that most people were smart enough to make such decisions. It was likely that he thought of himself as one of the smart ones! As you might imagine, Plato's ideas about politics weren't readily accepted.

WILL

NATURAL DESIRE

Plato wondered about humans, too. He thought that a soul was made of three parts: natural desire, will, and reason. Understanding our natural desires, having the ability to resist those natural desires, and knowing when to resist them was crucial to a balanced soul. Feeling thirsty is a natural desire. But if you are in the middle of giving a speech, your reason will tell you to wait until you have completed your presentation

REASON

before getting a drink. Your will makes waiting possible. Plato felt that a person who was unable to control the urges of natural desire had an imbalanced soul, which could lead to that person being bad.

Aristotle's Four Causes

The material cause: What is an item made out of?

The efficient cause: What is the source of motion?

The formal cause: What is the species? The kind? The type?

The final cause: What is the full development of the individual? What is the intended function of an invention?

Using this method, Aristotle might have followed this pattern of thought: a young whale is made of tissue and organs, which is the material cause. The efficient cause is its parents who generated it. Its formal cause is its species—whale—and its final cause is to grow into an adult whale.

Plato shared his ideas with students at a school he started in Athens called the Academy. During his time there, he continued to write about politics. He died at the age of 82. His students at the Academy are credited with writing down much of what they heard Plato speak of, so that we still have a record of his ideas today.

Aristotle (384–322 BCE)

Aristotle, another famous philosopher, was a student of Plato's. He combined philosophy and science by applying the Socratic method to

Logic

Wondering exactly what logic looks like? Look at this problem:

If Y is greater than 12, and 12 is greater than 2 then Y is greater than 2.

Make sense? Here's another: If London is in England, then London is not in China.

We know that London is in England. Therefore, London is not in China.

But what about this one: Jenny likes ice cream and Jenny likes broccoli. Therefore, Jenny will certainly like ice cream topped with broccoli.

Following this pattern of logic or reasoning can also lead to a conclusion that seems true, but is not.

the study of natural events. He questioned the causes of natural events, for example, the changes in weather and the motion of the tides. As he worked out his questions and answers, Aristotle developed the Four Causes. He made great progress in the fields of **biology**, **zoology**, **astronomy**, **physics**, **mechanics**, and many more.

words to know

biology: the science of life.

zoology: the science of animals, a branch of biology.

astronomy: the science of the celestial bodies, like the planets and stars.

physics: the science of matter and energy and their interactions.

mechanics: a branch of physical science that studies energy and forces in relation to solids, liquids, and gases.

premise: a condition stated at the beginning, something assumed.

inductive reasoning: the truth of the premises lends support to the conclusion but does not guarantee it.

deductive reasoning: the truth of the premises guarantees the truth of the conclusion.

logic: the science of formal, correct reasoning.

Sometimes he supported his arguments with research but in other cases his "data" was simply the current opinion about what was correct, or information based on what other people had previously written on a subject. Though his conclusions weren't always right, the method he developed—called **inductive reasoning**—is the foundation of the Western scientific method. Because of Aristotle's contributions to science, he is still considered by many to be the most important thinker of the entire Greek era, if not of all time.

One of Aristotle's greatest achievements was creating the field of **logic**, which is the study of correct reasoning. Before Aristotle no one had bothered to determine which arguments lead to true conclusions and which ones lead to conclusions that only seem true.

Know Your Ancient Greeks: Theophrastus (circa 370–285 BCE)

Theophrastus was born about 15 years after Aristotle, but when he enrolled as a student in Plato's Academy, the two of them quickly became good friends. They traveled around Greece and Asia Minor together, and when Aristotle died in 322 BCE, he gave Theophrastus his garden, library, and writings. At this time, Theophrastus also became director of the Lyceum, a school in Athens started by Aristotle.

Theophrastus ran the Lyceum for 35 years, doing research in all areas of botany, but also writing about superstitions—that is, irrational beliefs, like black cats causing bad luck. His work, *Characters* contains 30 humorous essays about different types of people, and it was so influential that European humor writers in the seventeenth century were still using it as an example of how to write. His other writing includes descriptions of minerals, gems, and rocks, and the experiments that Theophrastus and his students performed on them.

When Theophrastus died at age 85, he is believed to have said, "We die just when we are beginning to live." There's always more to research and discover, he thought, so we should never sit idle. In his words, "Nothing costs us so dear as the waste of time."

Architecture

7

THROUGHOUT GREECE TODAY, YOU CAN STILL FIND THE remains of buildings that were erected thousands of years ago. The ruins of enormous temples, such as the Parthenon, are still visible, making it easy to imagine the grandeur of these ancient sites. Archaeologists have also found remains of ancient Greek homes. Common Greek homes were fairly simple, and made of stone, wood, or clay bricks. However, the Greek temples and other public buildings were massive and beautiful.

Erecting these buildings was quite an endeavor. **Quarries** outside the city supplied the marble for the buildings. Masons used mallets and chisels to excavate the marble from the quarry. First they made grooves in the marble, and then hammered wooden wedges into the grooves. These wooden wedges were soaked with water, and as the wood absorbed the water, the wedges expanded, causing blocks of marble to crack apart.

Friezes

Most of the public buildings in ancient Greece were embellished with friezes. These elaborate scenes were carved from marble and ran around the building near the roofline. Sculptors carved these scenes in panels that were then mounted on the building.

The marble blocks were shaped roughly at the quarry, and then ox-drawn carts transported them from the quarries to the *polis*. Once the blocks arrived at the building site, expert carvers worked the blocks into their final form. They carved the blocks to fit together snugly. No mortar was necessary to cement the blocks into place, although they did use metal clamps to reinforce the building against earthquakes. Wooden **scaffolding** was built in order to lift the blocks of stone, roof tiles, and decorative elements into place.

To create **columns**, the stone carvers chiseled the marble into cylindrical shapes. These cylinders were round, but kind of short and squat—certainly not tall enough to be columns. To construct columns, workers pinned the marble sections together with metal pegs. Laborers then raised these heavy stone columns into position using ropes and pulleys. The ancient Greeks even had their own version of a skylight. The stone tiles on some roofs were partially transparent, allowing light to filter into the building.

Most—if not all—of the important public buildings in ancient Greece were embellished with at least one elaborate statue and a detailed **frieze**. Ancient Greeks painted these decorative elements with bright colors or highlighted them with tinted wax, but the wax and paints faded with time and are no longer visible.

words to know

quarry: an open area where marble and other rock is cut from the earth.

scaffolding: a temporary platform supported by a framework or suspended by rope that allows work at a great height.

column: a round pillar used to support weight in a building.

frieze: a carved band around a building.

You've already read about the Theatre of Dionysus with its tiered seating area and grand stage. Ancient Greece was also home to many elaborate public buildings, including gymnasiums, baths, and stadiums. But by far the most impressive were the temples.

Q: What is a frieze?

Temples

Each temple in ancient Greece was built in honor of a certain god or goddess. Initially, temples were built of limestone, but during the classical period (480–323 BCE) in ancient Greece, temples were more commonly constructed of marble. Temples were generally built in a rectangular shape. Early temples featured wooden columns at the front to support an extended roof.

Doric column.

Colossal Columns

- **Doric columns** are very plain. The top, called the capital, is a simple square. Doric columns were used frequently on mainland Greece and in the colonies in southern Italy.
- **Ionic columns** are more elegant than Doric columns. The shaft is a bit thinner and atop it is a scroll-like capital called a volute.
- **Corinthian columns** were used infrequently in ancient Greece. The capital is very elaborate and decorated with leaves.

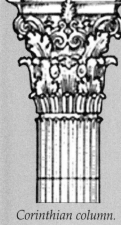

Corinthian column.

Ionic column.

Later, temples were built with a portico (kind of like a large porch) at the front and back, and long, open hallways along each side. Huge columns stood around the exterior of the building. These columns were stunning to look at, but they also served a purpose—to support the roof of the massive structure.

The Acropolis of Athens is the most recognized acropolis of the ancient world. It was fortified against attack and acted as a place of refuge for the citizens of Athens. As temples and public buildings were built, the Acropolis became the city's religious center and the focal point of public life. A stone staircase led visitors to the magnificent entrance of the Acropolis complex, the *Propylaea*. Beyond the entranceway stood the Parthenon along with two other temples: the Erectheum and the Temple of Athena Nike. Polished marble walkways between the three temples led visitors past towering statues and outdoor altars.

Q: What type of scenes were depicted on the **Parthenon's** frieze?

As you might imagine, most Athenians took great pride in their city and the amazing architectural accomplishments at the Acropolis. Athens was one of the most fabulous city-states in the ancient world and the elaborate complex made it all the more stunning.

The ruins of the Acropolis of Athens.

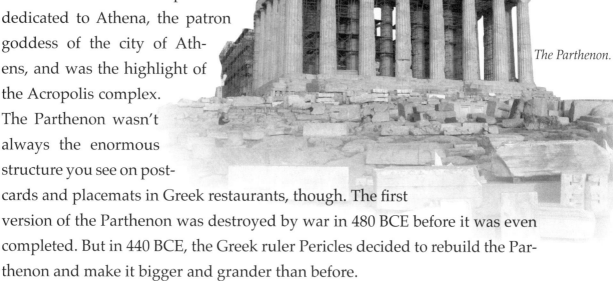

The Parthenon.

The Parthenon—the most famous of all Greek temples—was dedicated to Athena, the patron goddess of the city of Athens, and was the highlight of the Acropolis complex. The Parthenon wasn't always the enormous structure you see on postcards and placemats in Greek restaurants, though. The first version of the Parthenon was destroyed by war in 480 BCE before it was even completed. But in 440 BCE, the Greek ruler Pericles decided to rebuild the Parthenon and make it bigger and grander than before.

The Parthenon was 237 feet long, 110 feet wide, and 60 feet high. It was a rectangular building and had low steps up to the main floor on every side. A colonnade of Doric columns stood in line around the exterior of the building—there were eight columns along the short walls and 17 on the longer walls. There were six more columns at each entrance. The design of the Parthenon was a joint effort. The architect Ictinus planned the building and the sculpter Phidias, decorated it with sculptures and carvings.

The Elgin Marbles

At the turn of the eighteenth century, a British nobleman and diplomat named Thomas Bruce, the 7th Earl of Elgin, ordered that much of the Parthenon frieze be removed. He felt that the sculptures were being allowed to fall into disrepair, and wished to salvage them. Sometime between 1801 and 1805, the frieze panels—now known as the Elgin Marbles—were moved to Britain. Since that time, Greece and Britain have debated about who owns those marbles. Currently, they are on display at the British Museum in London.

Know Your Ancient Greeks: Pericles (circa 495–425 BCE)

Pericles was so influential in Athenian politics and culture that the time he was in power is often referred to as the age of Pericles. He became the recognized leader of Athens in 461 BCE, when aristocratic leader Cimon was ostracized for his friendship with Sparta. Pericles wanted all citizens to participate in matters of state, so he came up with a plan to pay them for participating. Pericles also worked to restore old temples and build new ones, including the Parthenon, and Athens became a center for literature and art.

Other Greek city-states came to resent the dominance of Athens, and Pericles himself. Some people claimed that Pericles used the taxes paid by all Greek city-states—collected for military protection—for improvements to the city of Athens. During the Peloponnesian War, Pericles moved people from the countryside to within the walls of Athens to keep them safe from the Peloponnesian army. When plague broke out in the overcrowded city of Athens, Pericles was blamed. He was removed from office and fined for misuse of public funds. Though he was later reinstated, he died of the plague soon after.

One sculpture depicted the birth of Athena and another, her rivalry with Poseidon, god of the sea. Around the outside of the building, the frieze depicted scenes of daily life in Athens as well as the council of the gods debating the creation of mankind.

For 15 years, the people of Athens worked together toward the completion of the Parthenon. Thousands of men—Athenians as well as other Greeks—worked on the building during that time.

The Erectheum was situated in the Acropolis complex near the Parthenon. Its unique feature was the Caryatid Porch, which is sometimes referred to as the Porch of the Maidens. Caryatids are statues that serve as columns. At the Erectheum, six stunning stone maidens act as columns on the porch, helping to hold up the roof. The Erectheum was dedicated to several gods, including Athena and Poseidon. It housed the Athenians' most sacred statue, Athena Polias (Athena, goddess of the city), which was made of wood.

Wonders of the World

Ancient Greek engineers and architects dreamed big. Not only did they create enormous statues, temples, and public buildings, they also created four of the seven "wonders of the ancient world."

Considered by the ancient Greeks and Romans to be the most fabulous creations of art and architecture, the seven wonders are the Hanging Gardens of Babylon, the Great Pyramid of Giza, the Statue of Zeus at Olympia, the Temple of Artemis at Ephesus, the Mausoleum of Halicarnassus, the Colossus of Rhodes, and the Lighthouse at Alexandria. Seven wonders were chosen because the number seven was considered lucky by the mathematician Pythagoras.

Zeus at Olympia.

Though all but one of these ancient wonders no longer exist, we know about them through the writings of ancient Greeks and archaeological discoveries. Archaeologists have found coins depicting these wonders and they've also discovered the remains of a workshop that belonged to Phidias, the man who sculpted the statue of Zeus at Olympia.

The portico on the Erectheum known as the Porch of Maidens.

The Statue of Zeus at Olympia was a magnificent temple dedicated to Zeus. Designed by the architect Libon in 450 BCE, the Athenian sculptor Phidias had the honor of creating the statue of Zeus himself. The statue was 20 feet wide at the base and 40 feet tall. Even though Zeus was seated on a throne, his head nearly reached the top of the temple. The statue was made of ivory and gold and decorated with ebony and precious stones. The temple building is believed to have been destroyed by an earthquake. The statue of Zeus was taken by wealthy Greeks to Constantinople (now Istanbul, Turkey), where it was eventually destroyed by fire in 462 CE.

The Temple of Artemis at Ephesus was built by Croesus, King of Lydia, around 550 BCE. Honoring the goddess Artemis, the Temple of Artemis at Ephesus was often described as the most beautiful building on earth. The temple was built entirely from marble and included 127 sixty-foot-tall columns. It also featured many works of art and four bronze statues of Amazons. Artemis was the goddess of hunting and wild nature, and the Amazons—an independent tribe of female warriors—lived in a way that would have pleased Artemis.

In 356 BCE, on the same day that Alexander the Great was born, the temple was burned down by Herostratos, a deranged man in search of fame.

Legendary Greeks: The Amazons

The Amazons were a mythical band of female warriors, ruled by Queen Hippolyte. They are said to have lived near the Black Sea and made trips to Asia Minor where they founded many towns. Amazons were as fierce as lions, and it is said that girls had their right breasts removed in order to draw their bows more easily. Amazons governed and survived without the aid of men, who were not even permitted in Amazon lands.

While we know them as mythical, scholars still debate the possibility that these women were real. Archaeologists have uncovered the remains of warrior maidens in an area of Siberia, giving them more to ponder.

Amazon warriors.

The Colossus of Rhodes was an enormous statue of the sun god, Helios, built on the island of Rhodes in 226 BCE. It had a base of marble and skin made from cast bronze secured to a framework of iron and stone. The finished statue was over 100 feet tall, nearly the size of the Statue of Liberty. Its thumb was so large that few people could circle it with their arms, and each finger was the size of most statues. An earthquake hit Rhodes 56 years after the statue was built, devastating the city and breaking the statue at its weakest point, the knee.

Ptolemy III Eurgetes of Egypt offered to pay for repairs to the monument, but the leader of Rhodes consulted an oracle who forbade them to erect a repaired statue. The statue lay in ruins until 654 CE, when the Arabs invaded Rhodes, disassembled the statue, and sold it to a Syrian. One story claims that it took 900 camels to transport the pieces.

The Lighthouse of Alexandria was built to protect the rugged shoreline near Alexandria, Egypt. The area was dangerous to ships that came too close to land, so around 300 BCE the commander of the city ordered construction of an enormous lighthouse to warn sailors that they were close to shore.

The architect Sostratus designed a lighthouse that was over 380 feet tall (equal to a 40-story building). It had a giant mirror on top that could reflect the sun's light up to 35 miles during the day, and lighthouse keepers kept fires burning at night. The lighthouse survived into the 1300s CE, when it was destroyed by earthquakes. It was never rebuilt.

Common Homes

While the public buildings of ancient Athens and other city-states were awe-inspiring, the homes of Greek citizens were simple in comparison.

In most cases, homes were rectangular in shape, with the narrowest side of the home facing the street. The homes of wealthier Greek citizens might have two courtyards. The front courtyard with its adjoining rooms was called the *andronitis*, or "court of the men," and the rear courtyard with its adjoining rooms was called the *gynaeconitis*, or "hall of the women."

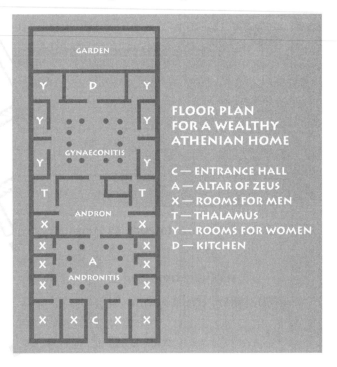

FLOOR PLAN FOR A WEALTHY ATHENIAN HOME

C — ENTRANCE HALL
A — ALTAR OF ZEUS
X — ROOMS FOR MEN
T — THALAMUS
Y — ROOMS FOR WOMEN
D — KITCHEN

The *andronitis* often had an altar at its center with a statue of Zeus the Protector. The courtyard might even be large enough to allow space for exercise. The *andronitis* acted as the living area of the home and was where the man of the house would receive visitors. Chambers used as storerooms or as sleeping spaces for male slaves or grown-up sons of the household were situated around this courtyard. Directly behind the *andronitis* was the dining area, called the *andron*.

Q: Name and describe three types of Greek columns.

The *gynaeconitis* was a courtyard similar to the *andronitis* and was hidden behind a door in the rear wall of the *andron*. Only the fathers, sons, and other close male relatives were allowed to enter this private space. Surrounding chambers included a kitchen, a room for working wool, and sleeping chambers for the female members of the household, including slaves. The *thalamus* was the bedroom that belonged to the master and mistress. This room had the most lavish furnishings and ornamentation in the house. At the rear of the home, there was likely a garden area for growing flowers or herbs and vegetables.

Shake and Bake

There are still many ruins in Greece where visitors can see the remains of ancient buildings like the Parthenon, the Olympic Stadium, and the Temple of Zeus. What happened to these buildings? Why are they in such disrepair?

The passage of time has a lot to do with it, but two other factors have also had an impact on the buildings raised so long ago: earthquakes and fire. Earthquakes have caused many stone pillars to come crashing down. These structures cannot withstand the earth-shaking that is common to Greece.

You might think that buildings made of stone would be safe from fire damage, but that's not so. Roofs of ancient Greek structures were supported by large timbers covered with tiles. If the timbers caught fire, the entire roof could come down. The stone itself could be damaged by fire, too. While stone will not burn, intense heat causes it to crack and crumble.

activity:
Craft a Column

Most of the major public buildings in ancient Greece featured columns. Add a little Greek style to your room by creating a column that you can use as a stand to display your favorite photos or trinkets.

1 Cut the cardboard tube to a 36-inch length. Wrap the corrugated cardboard around the tube so that the grooves run up and down. You can wrap it as many times as you like—the more layers you add, the sturdier and thicker your column will be. Add glue between each layer to hold it together and do your best to keep the ends even.

2 Trace around the bottom of the column in the center of both a small and medium-sized pizza box. Cut the medium-sized box so that there is a hole in the bottom of the box only. Cut holes in both the top and bottom of the small box.

3 Slide the column through the hole in the small pizza box, and then into the hole in the medium-sized box.

4 Use glue or tape to secure the column in the pizza boxes. These boxes will become the base of your column. Flip the column over and repeat the steps to add a top to your column.

5 Now, decide what type of column topper, or capital, you'll have—Doric, Ionic, or Corinthian. For a Doric column, you'll want to stick with just the two pizza boxes. For an Ionic or Corinthian column, use poster board to embellish and add details to your column. If you'd like, paint the column.

supplies

- ☒ **sturdy cardboard tube** (use one from a roll of gift wrap or visit a carpet store and ask for a tube from the center of a roll of carpet)
- ☒ **corrugated cardboard,** 36 inches wide
- ☒ **clean pizza boxes,** 2 small and 2 medium-sized
- ☒ **poster board**
- ☒ **glue or tape**

activity:
Make an Ancient Greek Building

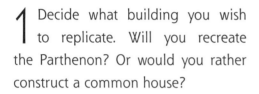

1 Decide what building you wish to replicate. Will you recreate the Parthenon? Or would you rather construct a common house?

2 Use cardboard tubes for columns, or make columns by rolling pieces of white paper into tubes. Cut the cardboard into pieces for the roof, the steps, and other parts of your structure.

supplies

- ☒ **some recyclables**, such as cardboard boxes, cardboard tubes, and bottle caps
- ☒ **glue and tape**
- ☒ **a sturdy, flat sheet of cardboard**
- ☒ **assorted craft supplies** such as pipe cleaners, construction paper, beads, etc.

3 Once you are happy with your structure, glue and tape the pieces in place onto the sturdy piece of cardboard.

4 Now, add details. If you are making a temple or other public building, add a frieze around the top of the building. You can glue on pipe cleaners or beads to make it three dimensional. Detail your columns with bottle caps, pipe cleaners, or beads. If you're crafting a common home, use bits of construction paper to add a mosaic pattern on the floor.

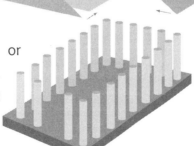

8 Science, Math, and Medicine

BEFORE THE SIXTH CENTURY BCE, THE GODS WERE considered responsible for things like illness and death. If someone experienced misfortune, surely they had offended the gods. If the seas raged, someone must have angered Poseidon. But over time the ancient Greeks changed their way of thinking and interpreting the world. They discovered explanations for events they had previously attributed to the gods. Their inquiring minds and interest in how the world worked led to some impressive scientific discoveries and inventions.

Although the ancient Greeks continued to believe in the gods, they began to understand natural causes. **Science**—the act of learning about the world through observation, identification, and experimental investigation—became an important part of ancient Greek life.

Greek scientists explored the **properties** of **matter**, developed **theories** about **atoms**, studied **anatomy**, and created medicine. They discovered and improved upon methods for moving cumbersome and heavy items, such as ships, building materials, and statues. They even made an ancient computer!

Archimedes's screw.

words to know

science: the study of the physical and natural world using observation and experiment.

properties: a quality or feature of something.

matter: any substance that takes up space.

theory: an idea about something, that explains why something is the way it is.

atom: the most basic, smallest particle of matter.

anatomy: the branch of science that studies the body.

Simple Machines

There are six types of simple machines: the lever, the wedge, the pulley, the wheel and axle, the inclined plane, and the screw. These simple machines were used long before people in ancient Greece began experimenting with them, but the curiosity of those ancient Greeks led them to use these simple machines to create more complex machines. One Greek famous for his inventions is Archimedes. Considered one of the greatest mathematicians of all time, Archimedes used his knowledge to invent devices like the Archimedes' claw, a catapult, and the Archimedes' screw.

Archimedes' inventions were inspired by his desire to solve the problems that people of his time faced every day. During a visit to Egypt, Archimedes invented his endless screw to help peasants bring water from the Nile to irrigate their fields.

He improved upon early water clocks by adding gears that showed the moon and planets in orbit. Water clocks are clay vessels made to slowly leak water, thus marking the passage of time. Archimedes also invented numerous weapons. These were used in defense of his birthplace, Syracuse, a Greek colony on the Italian island of Sicily, against the Romans.

Archimedes.

A Classical Computer

Among the most fascinating creations of ancient Greece is a complicated, computer-like device that was found by divers in 1901 off the southern tip of mainland Greece. The dials, gears, and inscribed plates were badly corroded after 2,000 years under water, but scientists believe that the device used gears connected to a hand-driven axle to mimic the movement of the sun, moon, and planets. In other words, the Greeks had created an **analog computer** of sorts for tracking the movement of heavenly bodies.

Named after the island it was found near, the Antikythera Mechanism remains something of a mystery. Nothing similar has been found. Knowing that the Greeks had such complex mechanical skills, however, makes scientists wonder what other surprises might be hiding beneath the waves.

The war weapons of Archimedes included catapults and the claw, a crane-like machine that lifted enemy ships out of the water and onto the rocks. His mirrors could concentrate the sun's light on enemy ships, setting them ablaze. Did these inventions really work? Scientists have experimented with the Archimedes' mirror and found that it might have worked, if the targets were in close range.

When working on a diffucult problem, Archimedes often became so involved with his work that he would forget to eat!

Atomic Knowledge

Just as ancient Greek scientists wondered about the cause of illnesses, they questioned what the world was made of. They made many discoveries in **physics**, the study of matter and energy. Many Greek philosophers believed that the world was made of particles, though they didn't agree upon just

words to know

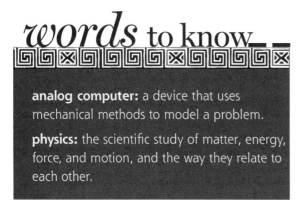

analog computer: a device that uses mechanical methods to model a problem.

physics: the scientific study of matter, energy, force, and motion, and the way they relate to each other.

how these particles worked. Some argued that there was a single basic element that made up the earth while others thought there were more. Some thought that all of these particles were exactly the same, and others guessed that every substance had its own kind of particle.

Around 400 BCE, a man named Democritus developed a theory about atoms. The word *atomos* means indivisible in Greek. He believed that atoms are so small that they are invisible to the eye, indivisible into smaller parts, solid with no empty space inside, and eternal because they are perfect. He also thought atoms were able to assemble in an infinite number of shapes. That's why the world has so many different objects in it.

Know Your Ancient Greeks: Democritus (circa 470–380 BCE)

Democritus is known mostly for creating the theory of atoms with his teacher Leucippus, but Democritus researched many other topics during his lifetime. Unfortunately, most of his writing was lost, but the works of other ancient Greeks shed some light on his accomplishments. He wrote about numbers, geometry, and mapping, and he was the first person to figure out formulas for the volume of a cone and a pyramid.

Supposedly, he traveled to Egypt, Babylon, India, Persia, Ethiopia, and many other lands to meet other thinkers. In addition to exploring zoology (the study of animals), botany (the study of plants), and medicine, Democritus had big ideas about the structure of the universe. He thought that the Milky Way was made of stars that were so far away that they blended together from our point of view. He also suggested that stars other than the sun had their own planets, probably with other living beings on them. Life on other planets? That's a theory we are still trying to prove today!

The Golden Crown

King Hiero II ruled Syracuse, a Greek colony on the island of Sicily, from about 270 to 215 BCE. During his rule, he commissioned a goldsmith to create a golden crown (likely for a statue of a god or goddess). The king gave the goldsmith a specific amount of gold to create the crown. But the king suspected that the goldsmith was deceitful and rather than crafting a solid gold crown, used less expensive silver to fill it. The crown, made in honor of the gods, was a sacred object and could not be melted down to check its purity.

The king brought this dilemma to Archimedes and asked him to figure out whether he had been cheated. Archimedes wasn't sure how to tackle this problem, until one day when he was taking a bath. He noticed that submerging his body caused the water to overflow. He figured out that the volume of water displaced is equal to the volume of the submerged item. With this knowledge he devised a plan. Archimedes knew that silver weighs less than gold. So the goldsmith would have had to use a greater amount, or *volume*, of silver to make a crown that matched the *weight* of the original piece of gold. Archimedes filled a container of water to the brim and put the crown in the water to measure its volume. He then repeated the experiment with a solid piece of gold exactly the weight of the one King Hiero II had given the goldsmith.

Archimedes discovered that the goldsmith—obviously less concerned with angering the gods than King Hiero II—had tried to trick the king by filling the crown with silver, thus making a dishonest profit. There's no record of what happened to the goldsmith, but you can be sure that King Hiero II was thankful for Archimedes's discovery.

What's more, argued Democritus, atoms move around freely in an empty space. This movement of atoms explains why some objects are hard and some soft, why you can see fog, yet put your hand through it.

Democritus's theory of atoms is similar to our modern view of atoms—but today's scientists didn't get their understanding of atoms from the Greeks. In fact, we only know of Democritus's ideas because the Roman poet Lucretius wrote down the theory of atoms in the second century CE, 500 years after Democritus died. Modern scientists believe that all atoms are the same, though they can differ in size and properties such as color and, when linked together, can create different elements.

Calculating Greeks

The ancient Greeks gave us a knowledge of physics, as well as many of the mathematical theories and formulas we still use today.

Knowledge about mathematics started out with the basics. Counting was likely created so that herdsmen could track their flocks of animals. We know this because archaeologists have found scratches carved in bones that are thousands of years old. It's hard to look at a bunch of scratches, though, and immediately see the difference between | | | | | and | | | | | |, which is what led to the creation of numbers.

Know Your Ancient Greeks: Pythagoras (circa 580–500 BCE)

The first real mathematician to emerge in ancient Greece was Pythagoras of Samos. In fact, he and his students are thought to have been the first to use the term *mathematike* to mean "mathematics." Before Pythagoras, *mathema* referred to any type of learning.

Pythagoras focused on clear thinking through "deductive reasoning"—that is, using basic principles and general laws to figure out specific facts and solve problems. He was so devoted to the study of geometry and arithmetic that he opened his own school, which also taught music and astronomy. Students had to live by strict rules so that they could develop pure minds and bodies.

One discovery that comes directly from Pythagoras and his students was the proof that the three angles of a triangle equal the sum of two right angles (180 degrees).

Pythagoras and his students developed very personal relationships with the natural numbers (1, 2, 3, etc.). They thought of odd numbers as male and even numbers as female, and they described numbers as beautiful or ugly, perfect or incomplete. Ten, for instance, was the best number because it was the sum of the first four numbers and could be written as dots in a pyramid to form a perfect triangle.

$$1 + 2 + 3 + 4 = 10$$

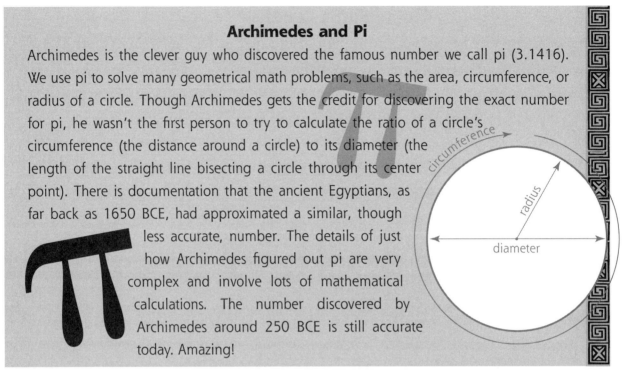

Archimedes and Pi

Archimedes is the clever guy who discovered the famous number we call pi (3.1416). We use pi to solve many geometrical math problems, such as the area, circumference, or radius of a circle. Though Archimedes gets the credit for discovering the exact number for pi, he wasn't the first person to try to calculate the ratio of a circle's circumference (the distance around a circle) to its diameter (the length of the straight line bisecting a circle through its center point). There is documentation that the ancient Egyptians, as far back as 1650 BCE, had approximated a similar, though less accurate, number. The details of just how Archimedes figured out pi are very complex and involve lots of mathematical calculations. The number discovered by Archimedes around 250 BCE is still accurate today. Amazing!

Different mathematical fields developed for various practical reasons. **Geometry**, for example, fulfilled a need for accurately measuring space. In the original Greek, geometry means "measurement of the earth."

Geometry may be a Greek word, but the study of measurement actually began in Egypt. Each year, the Nile River flooded, washing over the croplands, and each year Egyptians had to map out the fields to reestablish where one farmer's fields stopped and their neighbor's began. Geometry basics

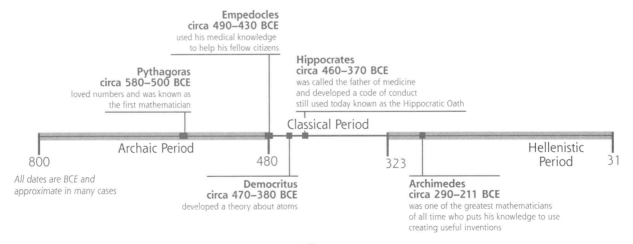

Empedocles
circa 490–430 BCE
used his medical knowledge
to help his fellow citizens

Hippocrates
circa 460–370 BCE
was called the father of medicine
and developed a code of conduct
still used today known as the Hippocratic Oath

Pythagoras
circa 580–500 BCE
loved numbers and was known as
the first mathematician

Classical Period

Archaic Period

Hellenistic
Period

800

480

323

31

All dates are BCE and
approximate in many cases

Democritus
circa 470–380 BCE
developed a theory about atoms

Archimedes
circa 290–211 BCE
was one of the greatest mathematicians
of all time who puts his knowledge to use
creating useful inventions

were brought from Egypt to ancient Greece by Thales of Miletus, who, on his return to Greece, further developed geometric theories. Thales went beyond asking *how* geometry

geometry: the measurement and relationships of points, lines, angles, surfaces, and solids, from the Greek *geo* (earth) and *metro* (measure).

worked and investigated *why* it worked. He realized that understanding how to measure crop lands and lay out cities and palaces is useful, but that knowing the general rules of geometry is even more valuable because then you can measure anything!

Ancient Remedies: Healing from the Heavens

According to Greek mythology, the centaur Chiron—half-man, half-horse—invented medicine so that he could heal himself after being wounded in a battle with the strong and courageous Heracles, son of Zeus. Chiron then taught the healing arts to the hero Achilles (whose mother dipped him into the River Styx, making him invulnerable to wounds), and to Asclepius, who was thought to be the son of the sun god, Apollo.

Chiron

Asclepius

A Staff of Snakes

Most ancient Greeks thought that snakes had healing properties, and Asclepius was always pictured with a snake wrapped around his staff. Why snakes? Perhaps because snakes shed their skins, which makes it seem like the snake is being reborn again and again.

Today, the caduceus—a staff wrapped with two snakes—is a symbol used by many modern doctors, but the caduceus was originally a symbol of Hermes, the quick-footed messenger god. Asclepius only ever had a single snake by his side, and really, isn't one snake enough for anyone?

Know Your Ancient Greeks: Empedocles (circa 490–430 BCE)

Empedocles was born into a very wealthy family in Acragas, a Greek colony on the Italian island of Sicily. As a boy he studied philosophy, natural sciences, and the arts.

As an adult, Empedocles used his medical knowledge and wealth to improve the welfare of his fellow citizens. When a plague infected the city of Acragas, Empedocles created a wall of animal skins to cover an opening in the city and divert the illness that was coming in on a polluted breeze. Later, in the neighboring city of Selinus, he diverted the course of two rivers to clean a polluted water supply and stop the spread of disease in the town. These accomplishments, as well as his writings on philosophy, made Empedocles quite famous, and he came to be treated something like a god. According to legend, Empedocles threw himself into Mount Etna, a volcano in Sicily, leaving behind one bronze sandal. A single bronze sandal was associated with Hecate, goddess of magic, and by leaving it behind, Empedocles indicated that he thought he was going to become immortal, a true god.

In fact, Asclepius was a human who lived around 1200 BCE, but his medical abilities were so respected that he was thought to be as powerful as a god.

According to one story, ancient Greeks overcame the pain of gout (a painful foot inflammation) by standing on electric eels until their feet were numb.

Nearly every Greek town featured an *Asclepieion*, a temple devoted to Asclepius where ailing citizens could rest, pray, sacrifice to the gods, and drink clean water. A sick person resting in the temple might either be healed by Asclepius or have a dream in which Asclepius would explain how the person could be healed.

One story tells of a man with a nasty sore on his toe who dreamed that a serpent crawled into the temple and licked his toe. When the man woke up, his toe was cured.

Greeks in the seventh and eighth centuries BCE knew a lot about anatomy—that is, the structure of the human body. Trainers at *gymnasia* knew how to treat injuries like sprains, fractures, and dislocations. Homer's *Iliad* describes bandage techniques, battlefield surgery, and the use of anesthetics (substances that numb part of the body) before almost anyone else performed these treatments.

Gruesome Lessons

As scientists became interested in medicine, they wanted to learn more about how the body worked on the inside. Without X-rays, the only way to see inside a human body was to dissect one. Some dissections were done on dead people or animals—but in other cases, a procedure called vivisection was used on condemned criminals. These criminals were cut open while they were still alive, allowing the surgeons to see the heart, brain, and lungs at work.

Ancient Greece in the third century BCE wasn't a good place to break the law!

Beyond anatomy, though, ancient Greeks generally didn't have much medical knowledge. They couldn't treat a cold properly and didn't really understand how the body worked. If a wound got infected, their only solution was to call in the snakes!

Hippocrates Gets Hip to Medicine

Despite medical theories that no longer hold true, good medical schools did develop in ancient Greece during the fifth century BCE. One of the most important schools was located at Cos, an island in the Aegean Sea, and another at Cnidus, both near present-day Turkey. The schools offered classroom lessons, research, and apprenticeship programs in which students worked side by side with teachers. Students had to promise to help the sick, to love humanity as much as they loved their work, and never to take a patient's life.

More than 2,400 years later, doctors and nurses still take a similar vow. We call that vow the Hippocratic Oath, after Hippocrates, the leader of the medical school at Cos.

Hippocrates became known as the "father of medicine." He wrote hundreds of papers on surgery, anatomy, diseases, treatment of illness with diet and drugs, and medical ethics—that is, the code of conduct that doctors should follow. He taught medical students to observe their patients carefully and record facts, a practice essential for good science. Even more importantly, he convinced most people that illness and disease had natural causes and weren't inflicted by angry gods.

Know Your Ancient Greeks: Hippocrates (circa 460–370 BCE)

Little is known about Hippocrates other than that he accepted money from patients in exchange for care and he taught medicine at the school on the island of Cos.

While his personal history may be a mystery, his influence on the world of medicine isn't. The Hippocratic Collection is a set of 60 medical textbooks that tell doctors how they should do their job. While Hippocrates didn't write every book—which is impossible since they were written over a period of 150 years—his method of practicing medicine is present on every page.

In the book *On Epidemics*, for example, the doctor learns to note specific symptoms in the patient on a day-by-day basis so that he can record the history of the illness. This practice will allow him to treat future patients better. In the book *On Forecasting Diseases*, the doctor learns what to look for in a patient—hollow eyes, cold ears, strange face color—so that he can ask the right questions. Another volume explains how to fix a dislocated shoulder and treat a bone fracture.

According to Hippocrates, the earliest Greek doctors spent too much time on philosophy and not enough time looking at the patient and his symptoms and learning from previous experience. Thanks to the teaching of Hippocrates, the way that doctors treat patients changed forever.

activity:
Stomachion

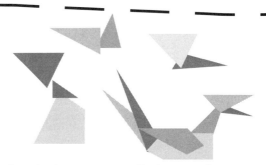

Archimedes explored the concepts of geometry by playing a game called Stomachion. Some records refer to this game as *loculus Archimedius* (Archimedes' box).

1 Use the pencil to lightly mark your square into 1-inch grids.

2 Duplicate the image you see below, using the grid to help you accurately place each line. Once you have the lines marked in pencil, trace the lines with a dark marker. Color the shapes in any manner you'd like.

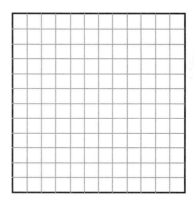

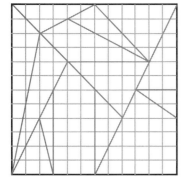

3 Cut along the dark lines to create a 14-piece puzzle.

4 To play, use all of the shapes to create clever pictures—like animals or structures.

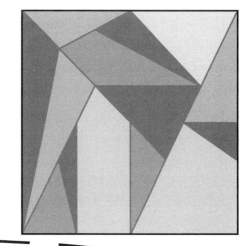

supplies

- ☒ **a 12-inch square of poster board**
- ☒ **pencil**
- ☒ **markers**
- ☒ **scissors**

activity:
Make an Abacus

Keeping track of things in ancient Greece was more difficult than it is today because they didn't have a numbering system that worked well yet. While hands and fingers helped in counting, there were times when a quantity was too large to use this method. To help in keeping track of items, they used a tool called an abacus.

1 Measure off and mark 10 equal increments along both long sides of the shoebox lid, making sure that the marks are directly across from each other. Punch a hole at each mark.

2 Cut the extra strip of cardboard to the same length as the shoebox lid. This will be glued into the lid as a divider. Punch holes in the strip of cardboard to align with those in the sides of the lid.

supplies

- ☒ **sturdy shoebox lid**
- ☒ **ruler**
- ☒ **hole punch**
- ☒ **strip of sturdy cardboard,** about 1 inch by 15 inches
- ☒ **glue**
- ☒ **about 10 wooden skewers,** 12 inches long
- ☒ **70 beads** (these must slide easily on the skewer)

3 Glue the piece of cardboard into the shoebox lid, about 2 inches from one of the long sides. Let the glue dry. The narrow section will be called the upper deck. The wider section is the lower deck.

4 Push a skewer through the first hole, into the lower deck. String five beads onto the skewer. Continue pushing the skewer through the divider, into the upper deck, adding two beads before pushing the end of the skewer through the last hole. Continue in this manner for all skewers. Glue the skewers in place at the sides of the box.

5 To use your abacus, place it flat on a table, with the lower deck closer to you. Push all the beads away from the divider. The beads in the upper deck are valued at 5; those in the lower deck are valued at 1. To use the abacus to count, move the beads in the far right column toward the divider. When you count five beads on the lower deck, you will carry to the upper deck. In other words, you'll move the five beads back to the starting position and move one of the beads from the upper deck toward the divider.

For instance, to count out the number eight, you will move one bead (5) from the upper deck and three beads (3) from the lower deck. Adding two (2) beads will give you all the beads on the lower deck, so you'll move those bottom five back (5) to the bottom and another from the top deck to the middle, which equals 10 (5 + 5).

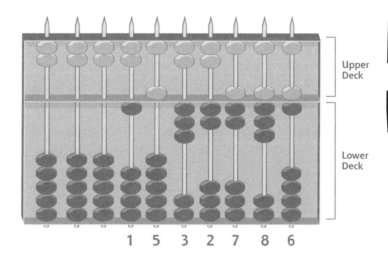

Upper Deck

Lower Deck

1 5 3 2 7 8 6

When you count both of the beads on the upper deck (reaching the number 10), you carry that information to the adjacent skewer—push one bead from the second column to the middle and both beads from the first column to the bottom. The skewer farthest to the right is the units or single digits column; the skewer adjacent to this, the tens column; the next, the hundreds column and so on.

101

9 Mapping the World and the Stars

JUST HOW DID ANCIENT TRAVELERS KNOW WHERE THEY WERE going? **Geography** didn't begin with the Greeks, of course. Sailors and traveling merchants from countries such as Egypt and Babylon mapped harbors and other locations essential to their work. But can you imagine how *different* each person's map would look?

Ancient Greek travelers seldom left sight of land, so there was little chance that they'd be lost at sea. Those sailors and traveling merchants did map harbors that they visited as they traveled, though, expanding on the information that earlier map makers had recorded.

Just as they did in so many other scientific fields, the Greeks turned a haphazard and scattered practice into a rigorous science, starting with Homer's epic work, *The Odyssey*. This story of Odysseus is known more for its adventure and battle scenes than its geographical research. But *The Odyssey* accurately describes much of the eastern Mediterranean coastline—and even includes the distances between many lands.

The Center of the World?

Anaximander of Miletus is thought to have created the first world map in the early sixth century BCE.

Odysseus' ship.

Since he knew Greece better than any other land, he naturally placed Greece in the center of the map, surrounding it with bits of Europe, Asia, and Africa. These land masses were circled by an ocean, so that the entire earth fit onto a tiny disc.

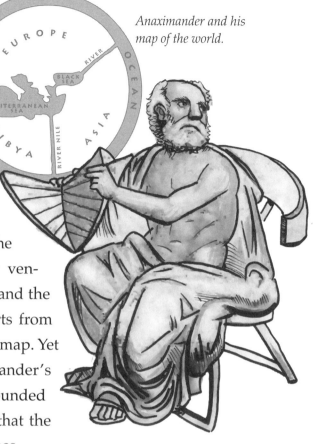

Anaximander and his map of the world.

Hecataeus, also of Miletus, improved Anaximander's map. He added many details to the coast, including the western parts of the Mediterranean Sea where the Greeks rarely ventured. In addition to traveling through Greece and the surrounding lands, Hecataeus relied on reports from traveling sailors for improvements to his world map. Yet even with this information, he repeated Anaximander's faulty portrayal of the earth as a flat disc surrounded by a single ocean. The first person to suggest that the earth was a globe was a man named Eratosthenes.

Where in the World is Ancient Greece?

It's important to know just where ancient Greece was on the map and how vast it was. The mainland of ancient Greece, situated on the Aegean Sea, looks very similar to modern-day Greece. At their most powerful, the ancient Greeks controlled mainland Greece, a large number of islands in the Aegean Sea, and parts of countries that are now Italy, Egypt, Spain, and Turkey.

Eratosthenes and the Deep Well

Eratosthenes (*circa* 275–195 BCE) was a Greek living in Alexandria, Egypt. Not only was he the first person to describe the world as a globe, he tried to measure it.

Eratosthenes knew that south of Alexandria, in the town of Syene, there was a deep well in which sunlight reflected off the water at the bottom of the well on one day of the year: June 21. On this day, and this day only, the sun was directly overhead at Syene. From living in Alexandria, Eratosthenes knew that the sun never appeared directly overhead in that city. However, the closest it came to being straight overhead was also on June 21, when the sun was 7.2 **degrees** away from being vertical. Eratosthenes knew this because he had measured the shadow made by a vertical stick in the ground on this day.

Eratosthenes thought about the shadows (and lack of shadows) created by the sun on June 21 and realized that the world couldn't be flat. If the world were flat, the shadows would be the same everywhere on the same date.

But what if the earth were round, like a ball? Then two sticks pointed straight into the ground in different cities wouldn't be **parallel**. Instead both sticks would point toward the center of the earth. With his knowledge of geometry, Eratosthenes knew that if you extended the sticks in Alexandria and Syene to meet in the center of the earth, the angle between them would be 7.2 degrees—one-fiftieth of a full circle. Eratosthenes measured the distance between the sticks at 5,000 *stades*. Remember this ancient Greek measurement from the chapter about the Olympics? If one-fiftieth of the earth is 5,000 stades, the entire **sphere** must measure 250,000 stades, equal to about 23,300 miles. The correct answer is 25,000 miles.

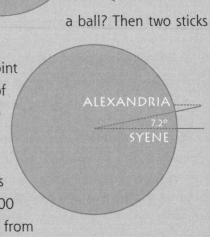

Eratosthenes's calculations enabled him to argue that the world was round, and to come amazingly close to estimating its size. Even so, more than 1,500 years passed before the concept of a round world was embraced.

Anaxagoras

Around 435 BCE, the Greek philosopher Anaxagoras suggested that the sun was a glowing rock larger than the 8,000-square-mile peninsula in southern Greece, the Peloponnesus. His claim went against the common belief that the sun was a god. He was imprisoned for **impiety**—it was feared that this outrageous claim might displease the gods.

As the ancient Greeks mapped the world, calculating distance, height, or angles, mathematics came into play. Many of these map makers were also mathematicians, and they developed concepts that were the beginnings of geometry. While not all of the theories held up over time, many of our geometrical calculations have their roots in ancient Greece.

The ancient Greeks contributed much to the world of science. They didn't use the word "science" to describe their efforts, though. The Greeks used other words, such as *philosophia* (love of wisdom), *episteme* (knowledge), and *peri physeos historia* (an inquiry into nature) to describe their activities.

Tracking the Stars

Just as geometry helped the ancient Greeks begin to map the world, it also helped them map the stars and planets. Noting that you saw a star in the sky isn't as important as noting exactly *where* in the sky you saw it. And the only thing better than recording where you saw the star today is noting where you saw it the next day and the day after that and the day after that. **Astronomy**—that is, the study of the movement of the stars and planets—requires a long-term approach.

words to know

geography: the science of the earth and its features.

degree: a unit of measurement. There are 360 degrees in a circle.

parallel: side by side, always the same distance apart.

sphere: a globe or object similar in shape to a ball.

impiety: a lack of respect for a god or religion.

astronomy: the science of the celestial bodies, like the planets and the stars.

Know Your Ancient Greeks: Thales

Thales was born around 624 BCE and was the first Greek philosopher and scientist. He thought that you could understand the world by searching for and finding its *physis*—that is, its underlying physical principle. Our modern word *physics*, which refers to the science of mechanics, is derived from the Greek word *physis*.

Thales argued that every bit of land—from beach to plateau to mountain—had formed naturally from the water, much the way dirt piled up beside the Nile River each year during the floods. This land formed a flat disc that floated upon the ocean, and the water of the ocean was also in the air all around us. The sun, moon, and stars floated across the sky on this water, then landed far out on the ocean and circled around to return to the east, where they would start again the next day.

But wait, there's more! For Thales, water wasn't just part of the environment. Everything in the world—every tree, every brick, every person—was also made from water. The earth, air, and all living beings had begun as water and eventually they would become water once again.

Why did Thales believe this? He never wrote anything down, so we're not exactly sure. But Aristotle, the philosopher who was born 250 years later, wrote that Thales noticed that everything living contains moisture, and even heat itself is caused by moisture. Water can change from solid to liquid to gas, so Thales thought that living beings must be made of water because they change forms over their lifetimes.

Thales's argument isn't that good, but it's still important because of what it leaves out: **supernatural** beings. Thales asked questions about the world and looked for answers in nature instead of in religion. The word *science* wasn't used as we know it for another 2,000 years, but Thales's way of thinking was the start of what we today call the "**scientific method**."

To really understand the heavens you need to study them for years, as well as use the records of others who have done so. But why would the ancient Greeks want to study the sky in the first place? By understanding that the sun, moon, and stars followed a certain pattern, the ancient Greeks could begin to predict

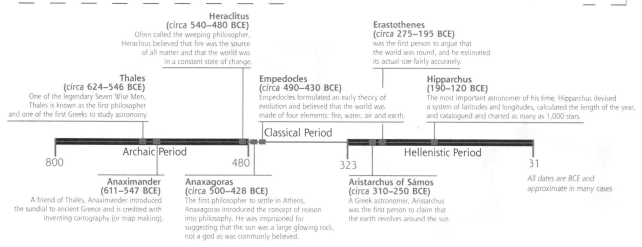

Heraclitus
(circa 540–480 BCE)
Often called the weeping philosopher, Heraclitus believed that fire was the source of all matter and that the world was in a constant state of change.

Erastothenes
(circa 275–195 BCE)
was the first person to argue that the world was round, and he estimated its actual size fairly accurately.

Thales
(circa 624–546 BCE)
One of the legendary Seven Wise Men, Thales is known as the first philosopher and one of the first Greeks to study astronomy.

Empedocles
(circa 490–430 BCE)
Empedocles formulated an early theory of evolution and believed that the world was made of four elements: fire, water, air and earth.

Hipparchus
(190–120 BCE)
The most important astronomer of his time, Hipparchus devised a system of latitudes and longitudes, calculated the length of the year, and catalogued and charted as many as 1,000 stars.

Classical Period

Archaic Period   Hellenistic Period

800   480   323   31

All dates are BCE and approximate in many cases

Anaximander
(611–547 BCE)
A friend of Thales, Anaximander introduced the sundial to ancient Greece and is credited with inventing cartography (or map making).

Anaxagoras
(circa 500–428 BCE)
The first philosopher to settle in Athens, Anaxagoras introduced the concept of reason into philosophy. He was imprisoned for suggesting that the sun was a large glowing rock, not a god as was commonly believed.

Aristarchus of Sámos
(circa 310–250 BCE)
A Greek astronomer, Aristarchus was the first person to claim that the earth revolves around the sun.

changes in season. This knowledge allowed farmers to plant crops at the most appropriate times and helped sailors recognize and predict safe and stormy seasons at sea.

Remember Thales, the clever Greek who bought all of the olive presses and made a fortune? He was one of the first ancient Greeks to study astronomy. He started by using information gained from other cultures. In his travels to Babylon, he ran across tables of astronomical **data** that recorded **eclipses** and the movement of the moon over the previous 150 years. From this data, he realized that eclipses occur roughly every 18 years. With this knowledge he successfully predicted an eclipse of the sun in 585 BCE.

The ancient Greeks had many stories for how the objects in the night sky came into being. They believed **constellations** represented mythological beings and the sun was the god Helios.

words to know

supernatural: magical or relating to a god.

scientific method: a system of gaining knowledge in a scientific way by formulating a question, collecting data through observation and experiment, and testing a theory or possible answer to the question.

data: factual information.

eclipse: when an astronomical object such as the sun or moon is partially or completely blocked from view by another astronomical object.

constellation: a group of stars forming a pattern or shape.

What's in a Name?

The word *planet* comes from the Greek language, but what does it actually mean? Greek astronomers noticed that most of the stars were in the same place night after night, but some stars moved. Greeks called these objects *asteres planetai* (wandering stars) or just *planetai* (wanderers), and the name stuck. The names we use for the planets today come from their Latin (or Roman) names. The Greek names sound different, but have the same meaning because each planet was named for the same god or goddess.

	Greek	Latin	English
Goddess of the earth	Gaia	Terra	Earth
God or goddess of the moon	Selene	Luna	Moon
God of the sun	Helios	Sol	Sun
God of knowledge or communication	Hermes	Mercurius	Mercury
Goddess of love	Aphrodite	Venus	Venus
God of death or war	Ares	Mars	Mars
God of the sky and storms	Zeus	Iuppiter	Jupiter
God of agriculture	Cronos	Saturnus	Saturn

But how the stars moved in the sky remained a mystery. Anaxagoras, a great thinker in Athens, suggested that the sun was not a god as many Greeks believed, but a burning mass of red hot metal. He was sentenced to death for this claim, but Pericles intervened, preventing the sentence from being carried out. Anaxagoras correctly described the sun and moon as separate objects and even suggested that eclipses are caused by the moon passing in front of the sun and the earth in front of the moon. His ideas were generally ignored.

Empedocles, a philosopher and statesman, suggested that the dark of night and light of day came from a sphere that rotated around the earth. This sphere was surrounded by a hard outer sphere on which the stars were fixed, creating a kind of star-studded dome above the earth.

Outer shell of fixed stars

Earth

Inner hemispheres of night & day

Empedocles' double sphere system of day and night.

108

To him, the sun and moon weren't physical objects, but merely polished spots on the inner sphere that reflected the light from the stars on the outer sphere.

words to know

geocentric: from the perspective of the earth as the center.

heliocentric: the sun is the center.

Going Around in Circles

Just as Greek map makers placed Greece at the center of the world, nearly every Greek astronomer thought that the earth was at the center of the universe. The sun, the moon, other planets, and the stars were all thought to circle the earth, which sat motionless.

There was a problem with this **geocentric** view of the universe, though. For one thing, the moon appeared to change in size during its cycle, which meant that either the moon was growing and shrinking (unlikely) or that the distance between the earth and moon changed with the seasons. The other planets known at the time—Mercury, Venus, Mars, Jupiter, and Saturn—also varied in brightness, which meant that the distance between them and earth must also change.

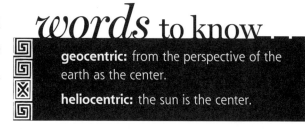

Geocentric view of the solar system.

The first ancient Greek to suggest a **heliocentric** view, that the earth rotated around the sun, was a man named Aristarchus. This suggestion was met with ridicule. Astronomers were convinced that the earth stayed in one place. ("Do you feel it moving? I don't feel it moving.") Hipparchus of Nicaea came up with a theory that worked remarkably well.

Heliocentric view of the solar system.

Using elaborate observations and calculations, he was able to determine the length of the year to within six and a half minutes. To do this, he kept track of the position of stars and how they related to the equinoxes. The equinoxes are the days of the year when night and day are equal in length, usually March 20 or 21 and September 20 or 21. He combined his observations with information recorded by people before his time to determine that a year-long cycle consisted of just over 365 days.

Two thousand years later, Aristarchus's idea was revived and further developed by the famous astronomer, Copernicus. It turns out that Aristarchus, the man ridiculed by ancient Greek astronomers, was right!

Aristarchus.

activity: **Ancient Greek City-State Travel Brochure**

An ancient Greek citizen from a distant colony who sees a map of Greece may wonder about some of the city-states on the map. Sparta? Athens? What might they find in such places? Here's your opportunity to explore that question. Use some of what you've learned about ancient Greece to design a travel brochure that would entice visitors to visit your favorite ancient Greek city-state.

1 Fold the paper into thirds. Determine how you'd like to lay out your brochure. Will you situate it horizontally or vertically? What will you put on the front?

2 Imagine that ancient Greece is still thriving. Describe the city-state of your choice, using rich descriptions that would make visitors want to stop at your destination. You can use a real city-state or make one up. Think about why someone might want to visit this particular city-state and be sure to share that information.

Pictures in the Stars

Constellations are groups of stars that resemble an object—the Big Dipper and the Southern Cross are two familiar constellations. To the ancient Greeks, constellations represented the heroes and heroines of ancient Greek mythology.

One constellation in the northern sky represents Cassiopeia. Her legendary boastfulness earned her a place in the sky, where she could be humiliated forever. How? The constellation appears to be upside down at certain times, which the ancient Greeks would have considered to be quite undignified. Near Cassiopeia is the

Andromeda.

3 Add details about some of the famous buildings and landmarks, as well as historical facts. What about the food, or events in your city-state?

4 Mention some of the famous Greeks that a visitor might meet in the agora and perhaps some entertainment that a visitor might expect to see.

5 Add pictures cut from old magazines or drawings of your own to illustrate the brochure.

Remember, your job is to sell visitors on the idea of traveling to this part of ancient Greece. You might not want to mention the lack of proper waste disposal or the smells that accompany it!

CHARIOT OF ZEUS
TOURS

TRAVEL WITH US AND
BE TREATED LIKE A GOD

TOURS OF ATHENS, ATTICA,
& TROY AVAILABLE

ASK ABOUT OUR
TROJAN HORSE SPECIAL

SENIOR CITIZEN DISCOUNTS AVAILABLE

supplies

Orion.

constellation bearing her daughter's name, Andromeda. This constellation appears to be a maiden held by a chain. Other constellations with ties to ancient Greek mythology are Pegasus, Orion, Heracles, the Centaur (which could represent Chiron) and Pleiades (also known as the Seven Sisters) representing the daughters of Zeus.

Q: Why did the Greeks **study** the **night sky**?

All of these constellations and more (there are 88 constellations recognized by astronomers) are still visible today. You might be surprised to learn, though, that these stars aren't in a fixed position. They do move. Because the universe is so vast, and these stars are so far away, they still appear very similar to the way they did when they were first discovered. Thousands of lifetimes will pass before there is a visible difference in these celestial pictures.

Legendary Greeks: The Boast of Cassiopeia

In ancient Greek mythology, Cassiopeia was the boastful and vain queen of Aethiopia. Her claim that she was equal in beauty to the blue-haired sea nymphs called Nereids angered the sea god Poseidon. In his wrath, Poseidon sent a giant whale to wreak havoc on Aethiopia. An oracle prophesied that the only way to stop the terror was to sacrifice Andromeda, the beautiful daughter of Cassiopeia and King Cepheus. Andromeda was chained to a rock on the shore, awaiting the monstrous whale when Perseus (just back from having slain Medusa) came to her rescue. Perseus and Andromeda wed, even though she was promised to Phineus. At the wedding, Perseus and Phineus quarreled and Perseus turned Phineus to stone with Medusa's head.

Warfare

ITH ALL OF THE ATTENTION THE ANCIENT GREEKS devoted to the arts, architecture, religion, and science, it's easy to think of Athens—and all of Greece—as a cultured city-state that loved living a fine life. But in reality, the ancient Greeks spent much of their time at war. It was common for city-states to fight for control over territory or argue about laws.

Athens seemed to be embroiled in battle constantly! The threat of war meant that citizen-soldiers had to be prepared to march off to battle at any time. Ancient Greek militiamen considered it a great responsibility to defend their community, traditions, and honor, and worked hard to stay in top shape.

There were a number of all-out wars that shaped the history of ancient Greece. Of course, the attack on the Greek Mycenaeans between 1200 and 1150 BCE was an important early battle, because it brought about the Greek dark age and then the beginning of ancient Greece as we know it.

The Trojan War—the battle that Homer tells us about in *The Iliad*—is another famous Greek war that was waged sometime during the twelfth or thirteenth century BCE. But over the years, other wars were just as important, making quite an impact on the history of ancient Greece. Two of the most important were the **Persian Wars** and the **Peloponnesian War**.

The Trojan War: Beware of Greeks Bearing Gifts

One of the most famous tales of ancient Greece is the invasion of the city of Troy. The Trojan War began when Helen, who some claimed to be the most beautiful woman in the world, was kidnapped and taken to Troy. Agamemnon, the leader of Mycenae and Helen's brother-in-law, called on the chiefs of the Greek tribes for support and sailed to Troy to retrieve Helen.

After 10 long and bloody years of fighting, the Greeks finally called it quits, left a giant wooden horse at the gates of Troy to apologize for all the trouble, and boarded their ships for home. The horse was the mascot of Troy, similar to how the bald eagle is the American national bird. Once the Greeks left, the Trojans pulled the wooden horse into their city to celebrate their victory.

Surprise! The wooden horse was actually filled with Greek soldiers. Once night fell, they snuck out of the horse and opened the gates of Troy, letting hundreds more Greek soldiers (who had only pretended to leave) overrun the city. Helen rejoined her husband, Menelaus, king of Sparta, for the long journey home.

For many years, historians weren't sure whether the Trojan War really happened, or even where Troy was! Since 400 years had passed between the Trojan War and the first written histories of its battles, a lot of *The Iliad* and *The Odyssey*—Homer's epic poems that include details of the war—may have been made up. But in 1871, the German archaeologist Heinrich Schliemann discovered ruins on the west coast of Turkey that archaeologists believe are the ruins of the ancient city of Troy.

Agamemnon.

Helen.

Trojan Horse.

Legendary Greeks: Odysseus

Following the Trojan War, Odysseus, the king of Ithaca, spent 10 legendary years trying to get back home. Odysseus's ships were cast onto the island of the Lotus Eaters, where part of his crew ate lotus leaves and fell into a trance from which Odysseus rescued them. They encountered the Circe, who with her magic potions turned part of the crew to pigs. They journeyed to the underworld where Odysseus communicated with the dead, and they were captivated by the Sirens who tried unsuccessfully to lure the crew to their death with melodious song.

Landing on the island of the Cyclopes, Odysseus and several of his men were trapped in a cave with the giant known as Polyphemus, who was the son of the sea god, Poseidon. When Polyphemus asked his name, Odysseus was wary. He cleverly answered, *"Outis,"* which means "nobody" in Greek.

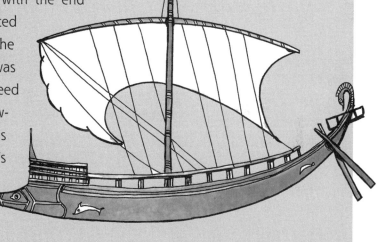

After several of his men were devoured by Polyphemus, Odysseus managed to blind him with the end of a tree trunk that had been heated in a fire. When Polyphemus told the other Cyclopes that "nobody" was hurting him, they didn't see any need to help. To escape from the now-blind Polyphemus, Odysseus tied his men to the underside of a sheep's belly and, even though Polyphemus ran his hand over the back of each sheep as it headed out to pasture, he was unable to detect the escaping men.

Returning to sea, Odysseus struggled with the wrath of Poseidon, who was furious that Odysseus has harmed his son. Repeatedly blown off course, Odysseus's ships were wrecked and eventually his entire crew perished. Odysseus finally managed to make it home, to find that his wife Penelope had waited for him, turning down offers of marriage for 20 long years.

You can read about all of Odysseus's adventures in Homer's *Odyssey*.

Heinrich Schliemann and the Lost City of Troy

As a young boy, Heinrich Schliemann was fascinated with the ancient Greeks. The stories of Homer, in particular, intrigued him and continued to do so throughout his adult life. Having made a good living as a representative for a Dutch shipping company, in 1866, at the age of 44, he retired and set out to follow his passion. He studied ancient Greece, determined to find the lost city of Troy. But Schliemann was not a trained archaeologist, just a passionate amateur. When he claimed that Troy was likely situated at the site of the city of Ilion, far from where professional archaeologists placed it, he was mocked. But, he was determined.

When Schliemann finally gained permission to excavate the site in 1871, he unearthed Hellenistic inscriptions and what appeared to be a Council House. He was convinced that he had located the lost city of Troy. Over the course of the next two years, he and his crew (including his wife Sophie) managed to excavate what appeared to be several cities that had been erected at different times.

When he suspected that he was close to finding a treasure, he sent the crew home and continued to dig with only Sophie at his side. Together they found a copper cauldron, gold jewelry and buttons, daggers, tools, and weapons. He discoverd vases made of bronze, silver, and gold. One particular engraving led Schliemann to believe that the treasure was that of King Priam, the ruler of Troy during the Trojan War.

In an attempt to prevent the Turkish or Greek governments from claiming ownership of the treasure, Schliemann smuggled his find out of the area, and divided it for safekeeping at the homes of friends all over Greece.

By 1879, the second city of Troy—likely built atop the ruins of the famous city of Troy—was found, as well as the palace of Priam that once stood in the ancient city of Troy. Schliemann died in 1890 and never saw the completion of the project that he so boldly began. From 1932 to 1938 an expedition from the University of Cincinnati unearthed what they felt was the Troy made famous in Homer's *Iliad*.

Some archaeologists question the discoveries of Schliemann, but others credit him and his great passion for history with helping discover the mysterious city of Troy.

Seven Cities?

The excavation at Ilion, the site of the ancient city of Troy in modern-day Turkey, unearthed seven different cities on the same site. How can this be?

When a city falls into ruin, the buildings may no longer be of value, but the land is still usable. If another group of people comes along and decides that they like the location, they might build on that same site. But the first city has already left its mark on the land, maybe with stones stacked in a certain way or a pot that was discarded and eventually covered with soil.

This is what happened at the site of the ancient city of Troy. Different civilizations thrived—cities were built, fell into disrepair, and then new generations rebuilt. So when archaeologists excavate a site, they find remains from different times in history buried in layers of rock and soil, called strata.

The Persian Wars

In their quest to conquer the world, in 546 BCE the Persians defeated King Croesus, ruler of Lydia, which is in present-day Turkey. Over several decades the Greek city-states of the area gradually came under the control of the Persian king, Darius I. The Persians appointed a man named Aristagoras to rule the Greek city of Miletus, which had been under Lydian rule. But Aristagoras didn't like Persia's strict rules, and in 499 BCE he organized a democratic rebellion, called the Ionian rebellion. He went to mainland Greece for support.

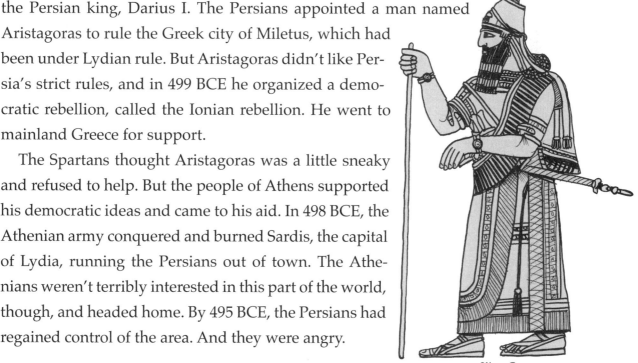

The Spartans thought Aristagoras was a little sneaky and refused to help. But the people of Athens supported his democratic ideas and came to his aid. In 498 BCE, the Athenian army conquered and burned Sardis, the capital of Lydia, running the Persians out of town. The Athenians weren't terribly interested in this part of the world, though, and headed home. By 495 BCE, the Persians had regained control of the area. And they were angry.

King Croesus.

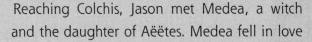

Legendary Greeks: Jason and the Argonauts

Jason, who was the true son of King Aeson, was brought up by the centaur Chiron far from court. During this time, King Aeson's half-brother, Pelias, took over the throne.

When he became a grown man, Jason went to court to claim his right to the throne. On his way, Jason met an old woman near a flooded river. She begged him to carry her across the water. Jason did, and lost a sandal in the process. The old woman was the goddess Hera in disguise, and Jason's good deed earned Hera's respect and devoted help.

Jason couldn't have known that Pelias had been warned about a threat to his throne that would come wearing only one sandal. Pelias was wary, and agreed to name Jason to the throne if he retrieved the golden fleece belonging to the cruel king of Colchis, named Aëëtes. With the help of Athena, Jason built his ship, called the Argo. He assembled his crew, the Argonauts, and headed off in search of the golden fleece.

Reaching Colchis, Jason met Medea, a witch and the daughter of Aëëtes. Medea fell in love with Jason and helped him to steal the golden fleece. Jason returned home with Medea, who killed Pelias. But Jason did not claim the throne as he had intended. Instead he lived with Medea for 10 years in Corinth before rejecting her and marrying King Creon's daughter, Glaucis. Jason lived to an old age and died when he was crushed under the prow of the Argo.

The Persians wished to punish Athens for the destruction of Sardis. In 490 BCE the Athenian and Persian armies met in the Battle of Marathon, perhaps one of the most important battles in Greek history. Marathon was a town northeast of Athens. King Darius sent 25,000 men to land at the bay of Marathon, and from there the soldiers were to march over land to Athens.

Nearly caught by surprise, the Athenians hurried to prepare. A Greek general named Miltiades knew something about Persian battle tactics, and formulated a plan. He felt it best to initiate an attack, rather than wait for the Persians to act. He placed a long line of men across a narrow valley, with the weakest formation at the front. The front formation was flanked on each side by two wings of capable soldiers—but they were hidden from view.

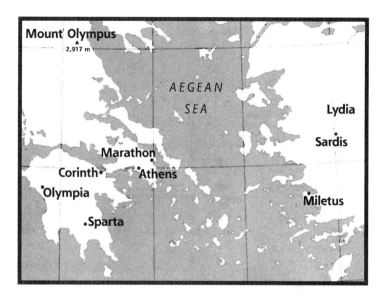

The Persians eagerly attacked the weak front and were immediately surrounded by the hidden Greek soldiers. In vicious hand-to-hand combat, the Persians lost 6,400 men. The Athenians lost only 192. These Athenian soldiers were buried in a common grave on the battlefield. The burial mound is still visible to those that visit modern Greece.

Despite the defeat of the Persian army at the Battle of Marathon, one Greek politician, Themistocles, convinced the Athenians that Persia wasn't done with them. Under the guidance of Themistocles, Athens amassed a fleet of over 300 ships by 481 BCE. In the same year, Persia's new king, Xerxes, assembled 150,000 men and a navy of 800 ships, determined to defeat the Greeks once and for all.

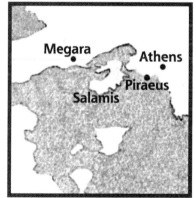

Strait of Salamis.

Themistocles knew that the battle could only be won at sea. The Greeks filled their boats with men skilled in hand-to-hand combat, then lured the Persian ships into the narrow **strait** between Salamis and Attica. When the Persians sailed into the strait they were trapped.

Themistocles.

Legendary Greeks: Theseus

The sea god Poseidon gave a snow white bull—the Cretan Bull—to King Minos of Knossos on Crete. When Minos refused Poseidon's instructions to sacrifice the bull, Poseidon made Pasiphaë, King Minos's wife, fall in love with the bull. She gave birth to the beast we call Minotaur, with the body of a man topped by the head of a bull. Minos ordered that a labyrinth (or maze) be built to contain the Minotaur. While the Minotaur was trapped in the maze, Poseidon released the Cretan bull, allowing it to terrorize the city of Marathon. A man named Theseus killed the bull, saving Marathon from much damage.

Stuck with the Minotaur, King Minos demanded a tribute of youth from the city of Athens to be fed to the Minotaur each year. Theseus was determined to stop this sacrifice and went to Crete to slay the Minotaur. With the help of Ariadne, King Minos's daughter, he succeeded in slaying the beast and escaping from the labyrinth. With his bravery, Theseus became one of Athens's most famous heroes.

At the Battle of Marathon, many soldiers claimed that they saw the famed Theseus running ahead of them, leading them to battle against the Persians.

There was not enough room for the ships to maneuver and flee. The Greek navy succeeded in sinking about 300 Persian ships before the rest of the Persians managed to escape. Following this disgraceful loss, Xerxes returned to Persia, leaving a small army of soldiers in Greece to try, yet again, to conquer Athens. They were unsuccessful.

Even though fighting continued between the Greeks and the Persians until 449 BCE, the Greek victory in the Battle of Salamis is important because it allowed the Greeks to avoid becoming part of the rapidly expanding Persian Empire. Greek culture might not have thrived if they'd lost their independence to Persia.

Xerxes.

Marathon Runner

As the story goes, when General Miltiades led the Greeks to victory over the Persians in the Battle of Marathon, he ordered a runner to carry news of the triumph back to Athens. This runner, Pheidippides, ran approximately 25 miles from the city of Marathon to Athens, shouting, "Rejoice, we conquer!" to all he passed. After having run that far without water or rest, he dropped dead. The modern marathon is based on this legend.

The Peloponnesian War

During the Persian Wars, the people of Athens wanted to make certain that they were always prepared for battle. They invited neighboring city-states to become their allies. They wanted partners who would help each other if they were attacked by the Persians. This **alliance** of city-states formed in 478 BCE was called the **Delian League**, because the group's headquarters were based on the island of Delos.

words to know

Persian Wars: a series of wars between Persia and the Greek world between 499 and 449 BCE.

Peloponnesian War: wars between the Greek city-states of Athens and Sparta that weakened both powers.

strait: a narrow channel of water connecting two larger bodies of water.

alliance: a group whose members agree to help each other.

Delian League: a military alliance of Greek city-states dominated by Athens.

There was just one problem. Not every ancient Greek city-state wanted to join this alliance. Those that were reluctant to join were eventually forced to become allies, but they were treated poorly by the league for their initial hesitation. Some city-states felt frustrated with Athens' domination of the league. Others believed that the fancy Athenians were using money from the Delian League treasury to improve the glorious city of Athens and rebuild temples destroyed by the Persians, rather than for protecting Greece from attack.

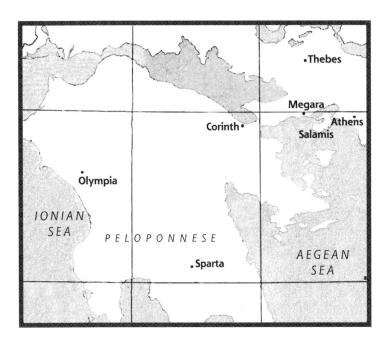

Under Pericles, the ruler of Athens, the Delian League became more like a dictatorship than a partnership. City-states that wanted to leave the league were not allowed to do so, and were viewed as traitors.

In one instance Athens attacked Thasos, an island off the northeast coast of Greece, to teach them a lesson. Their war ships were confiscated and their defenses torn down in an attempt to get Thasos to join the Delian League. The **Spartans**, leaders of their own military alliance, called the Spartan Alliance or **Peloponnesian League**, didn't like how bold the Athenians had become.

Athens and Sparta didn't always see eye to eye. They had a healthy respect for each other, but they were what we might call rivals today. Two of the biggest and most influential city-states, they each had a large army. Even so, they managed to live peacefully as neighbors for a long time.

Under the rule of Pericles things changed. The Delian League became more like an Athenian empire. When Athens forced Megara, a city-state directly between Sparta and Athens into the Delian League, Spartans became very uneasy.

Pericles.

words to know

Spartan: someone from Sparta. The word has come to mean simplicity, avoidance of comfort and luxury, and strict self-discipline.

Peloponnesian League: a military alliance of Greek city-states dominated by Sparta.

Legendary Greeks: Achilles

Achilles was born to a sea nymph named Thetis. Certain that Achilles was destined for greatness, but worried for her son's safety, as most mothers would be, Thetis took a precaution. She dipped baby Achilles into the River Styx to protect him from wounds. But as she dipped the baby, one part of his tiny body remained dry—his heel.

Under the care of the centaur Chiron, Achilles learned to be brave, to ride horses, and to hunt. Greece was preparing to go to battle with Troy, and the Greek army knew they needed Achilles in order to win the battle. After all, it had been prophesied that without Achilles the Greeks could not win.

Thetis had heard the prophecy, too, and took it upon herself to hide Achilles. She dressed him up as a girl and sent him to a faraway town. But clever Odysseus sent a gift to the "girl"—and when she expertly took up the spear and shield, she was recognized as Achilles and led off to the battlefield.

In the final year of the war, Achilles killed Hector, the prince of Troy. While dying, Hector swore that Achilles would die at the hands of Paris. He was right. Paris fired an arrow and hit Achilles directly in the heel. This was the one part of his body that didn't have the protection of the River Styx, and the wound killed him.

The expansion of Athens into Megara sparked one of the first clashes between Athens and Sparta, in 457 BCE. When Megara revolted in 446 BCE, Athens lost a buffer between itself and Sparta, meaning the Spartan army could appear at any time. Fighting between Athens and Sparta became common, but Athenians felt safe in their walled city, and a truce in 445 BCE brought some peace between the two powerful city-states. By 433 BCE the two powers were again provoking each other and it didn't take long before outright war broke out.

The Women of Sparta

Unlike girls in most Greek city-states, Spartan girls and women were encouraged to exercise and compete in athletic events. It was thought that a strong, athletic woman would give birth to healthier children. And healthy boys in particular made Spartans happy.

Despite the power of the Athenian navy, Pericles knew that Athens was no match for Spartan warriors. He kept his people safe within the walls of Athens, and let those remaining outside the city walls battle Sparta. He was content to let the Spartan warriors wear themselves out in campaigns that made little difference in order to save the lives of the many citizens sheltering inside the city walls. While there were losses outside the city's gates, they paled in comparison to the losses that Athe-

Q: What was different about the Peloponnesian War?

nians might have seen had they not taken refuge within the city. But Pericles hadn't counted on a plague. Illness in Athens killed many citizens—including Pericles himself.

The new Athenian rulers had different ideas—they left the safety of the walled city, and attacked the Spartan warriors. The Peloponnesian War was an on-again, off-again war, pitting Athens against Sparta in many different battles over many years.

Sparta finally won the war in 404 BCE. The Athenian naval fleet was destroyed, preventing them from reaching their source of grain across the Black Sea, and Athens starved. The Spartans demanded that Athens submit to

Alexander the Great.

rule by Sparta, tear down their defensive walls, and hand over all but 12 of their ships. While Sparta may have conquered Athens, after such a long and grueling war Sparta's army was also much diminished. Neither Athens nor Sparta ever returned to the power and fame they once knew and both slowly declined over the following century.

Alexander the Great

Macedonia lies to the north of the Greek mainland. Though the Macedonians spoke the Greek language, and Macedonia was inhabited by some Greek people, the mainland Greeks considered them to be uncultured and barbaric. But don't tell that to Alexander the Great.

Born in 356 BCE, he grew up watching as his father, King Philip II of Macedonia, did his best to conquer neighboring Greek city-states. King Philip knew that eventually Alexander would become king, so he made certain that his son was suited to the task. He hired the great Greek philosopher Aristotle as Alexander's tutor, and Alexander learned philosophy, geography, botany, and zoology.

King Philip II of Macedonia.

By the time Alexander was 16, King Philip had conquered all of the mainland Greek city-states except Athens, Sparta, and Thebes. Alexander joined his father's army of Macedonians and Greeks as it prepared to invade the Persian Empire. First, in order to present a united front against the Persians, King Philip's army needed to defeat Athens and Thebes, thereby securing their help in battle. The battle at Chaeronea against the two city-states in 338 BCE was Alexander's first battle and it ended quickly in favor of the Macedonians.

By 337 BCE, all of the Greek city-states except for Sparta had joined with Macedonia to form the **League of Corinth**. King Philip died the following year, and at 20 years of age, Alexander became the king of Macedonia.

Q: What enemy was able to get through Athens' wall and kill Athenians well before the **Spartans** did?

Determined to carry out his father's plans, Alexander led his army to battle against the Persians. The Battle of Granicus was fierce but Alexander was victorious. During one exchange, a Persian soldier raised his sword to stab Alexander. With a single blow, the king's friend, Cleitus, cut off the attacker's hand. They watched as it dropped to the ground, still holding the sword.

With the success of that battle to bolster his image, Alexander and his troops traveled through Ionia. They were welcomed with open

Q: How did **Sparta** finally **defeat Athens**?

Coin from Alexander the Great.

arms in this region that is now Turkey. The city of Miletus resisted, and was conquered, as were other Persian cities along the coast. Weak from battle and unable to collect supplies, Persia finally surrendered around 332 BCE.

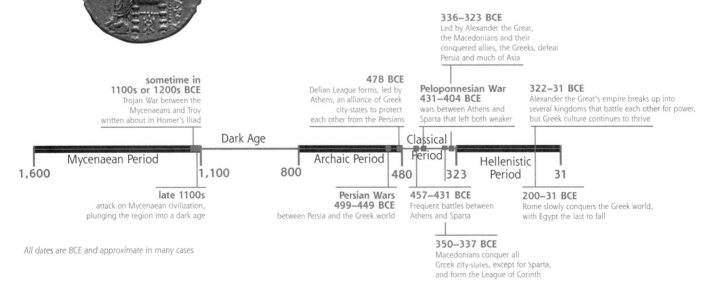

336–323 BCE
Led by Alexander the Great, the Macedonians and their conquered allies, the Greeks, defeat Persia and much of Asia

sometime in 1100s or 1200s BCE
Trojan War between the Mycenaeans and Troy written about in Homer's Iliad

478 BCE
Delian League forms, led by Athens, an alliance of Greek city-states to protect each other from the Persians

Peloponnesian War 431–404 BCE
wars between Athens and Sparta that left both weaker

322–31 BCE
Alexander the Great's empire breaks up into several kingdoms that battle each other for power, but Greek culture continues to thrive

Dark Age

Classical Period

| Mycenaean Period | | Archaic Period | | Hellenistic Period |

1,600   1,100   800   480   323   31

late 1100s
attack on Mycenaean civilization, plunging the region into a dark age

Persian Wars 499–449 BCE
between Persia and the Greek world

457–431 BCE
Frequent battles between Athens and Sparta

200–31 BCE
Rome slowly conquers the Greek world, with Egypt the last to fall

All dates are BCE and approximate in many cases

350–337 BCE
Macedonians conquer all Greek city-states, except for Sparta, and form the League of Corinth

The Great

Alexander was well respected by his soldiers and managed to lead his army across 22,000 miles of land without losing a single battle. He handled the people he conquered with grace, sharing the belief that people of different cultures could live together under the same government. It's no wonder that by the time he died at age 33, he had garnered enough respect that future generations would know him as Alexander the Great.

Alexander and his army stormed their way across Persia and Asia, conquering city after city. Before one battle, Alexander equipped the wheels of his chariots with curved knives meant to slash the legs of his enemy's horses and soldiers. Whenever he could, he situated his army so that the enemy was forced to approach over very rocky ground. He even had workers smooth out the ground where his army would take a stand. Alexander's clever thinking and the brute force of his army led him to success after success.

In 326 BCE, at the age of 30, Alexander led his troops against King Porus of India in the Battle of Hydaspes. Alexander came to battle with 700 horses. Imagine his surprise when he saw that King Porus's cavalry was made up of 200 elephants! In spite of the elephants, Alexander was again the victor and from that time on, he had his own cavalry of elephants in battle.

Preparing for Battle

The Greeks depended upon their citizens to serve in the military, and most of these middle-class men served as **hoplites**. Armed with spears, which were easy to maintain and affordable, hoplites fought shoulder to shoulder in a formation called a **phalanx**.

words to know

League of Corinth: a military alliance of all the Greek city-states except Sparta, led first by King Philip of Macedonia and then his son, Alexander. The alliance lasted until Alexander's death in 323 BCE.

hoplite: a foot soldier in ancient Greece armed with a sword and a spear.

phalanx: rows of soldiers marching tightly together with their shields joined.

cuirass: a peice of armor covering the body.

During battle, they used shields made of oak covered with leather or bronze to protect themselves from injury. A hoplite wore a bronze helmet, **cuirass**, and thin bronze plates strapped around bare legs. Sometimes a leather apron was hung from the lower part of the shield as added protection for the legs. The hoplites' weapons were handheld: a spear and a sword.

Weapons of War

Hoplites were skilled in hand-to-hand combat. But why get close to opponents and risk getting hit if you can strike them from far away?

Other wartime inventions include the catapult, created in 399 BCE by Dionysius, the elder of Syracuse. He was a cruel tyrant who made Syracuse the most powerful of the western Greek colonies. Catapults were built to hurl heavy objects or arrows over long distances, hopefully striking opponents. Flame throwers were another Greek creation, although they weren't guns that shoot out flames like you see in the movies. Instead, the Greeks filled pots with burning sulfur (a flammable mineral), tree sap, and other materials, then threw them onto the decks of enemy ships to set them on fire.

Catapult.

Weapon technology was an active field of innovation for Greek thinkers even after the Greeks lost their independence to the Macedonians and later, as they resisted the Romans.

Another tool for warfare was known as Archimedes' claw. The claw was actually a crane built into the battlements that surrounded and protected a city that could move large enemy ships close to shore, and destroy them as well! To do this, soldiers would hurl the claw hooks of the crane onto the front of an enemy ship. A team of oxen would then pull

A hoplite.

a series of ropes that lifted the crane's arm, pulling the front of the ship out of the water. Once the oxen pulled the ship as high as they could, the soldiers would suddenly drop the boat, either sinking or breaking it.

Even stranger than the ancient Greek flame throwers were their land-mines. Philo of Byzantium, who wrote much about ancient weaponry, described the mines around 120 BCE. He recommended that cities take empty earthenware jars, fill them with seaweed or grass, bury them around the walls of a city, and cover them with dirt. The mines supported the weight of the troops

Archimedes' claw.

that walked over them. But if an enemy tried to move in a heavy battering ram, the jars would collapse, causing the battering ram to sink into the ground. This made it impossible to move it any further and therefore, useless.

The End of Ancient Greece

After Alexander the Great died, his huge empire broke apart into smaller empires marked by wars and shifting alliances: Macedonia, Syria, and Egypt. Greek culture continued to thrive and spread, though, especially in Alexandria, Egypt. During the Second Punic War (218–207 BCE) between Rome and Carthage, King Philip V of Macedon allied with Carthage (a city in North Africa) to protect supply lines from the Roman navy. Rome saw Macedonia's participation as an invitation to interfere on the Greek mainland.

Coin from Alexander the Great.

Hoplites

Hoplites were bound by the rules of war called the *nomima*. In ancient Greece, war prisoners were entitled to fair treatment by their captors. Until the Peloponnesian War city-states would usually just swap prisoners after a battle. But the Peloponnesian War was brutal and the rules of war were often ignored.

We have something similar in the world today. Countries that abide by the agreement made at the Geneva Convention guarantee that their military will provide humane treatment to prisoners of war. Signed in 1864, it was the first treaty of international humanitarian law.

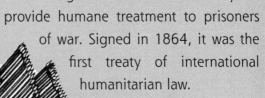

A phalanx.

From the time of the Second Punic War until about 146 BCE, there were numerous battles for control of the area around the Aegean Sea. In 146 BCE, Rome conquered the Achaean League—the last group of Greeks living independently of the Roman Republic—ending the independence of ancient Greece as a whole. In the same year, the Battle of Corinth completely decimated the Greek city-state of Corinth.

Even after Rome defeated the Greeks in the Battle of Corinth, many Hellensitic kingdoms remained devoted to the Greek way of life. The last Hellenistic kingdom to fall to Rome was Egypt, under the rule of Cleopatra, in 31 BCE. Greece came to be a province of the Roman Empire and remained under Roman control until the thirteenth century CE.

According to legend, Archimedes, the inventor and mathematician who lived in the 200s BCE, developed giant reflecting mirrors that focused sunlight on Roman ships as they attacked Syracuse, setting the ships on fire.

activity: **Labyrinth**

Create a small-scale labyrinth of your own and see if you can rescue a marble from its twists and turns.

supplies

1 Press the clay into the shoebox lid, making the surface as smooth as possible. The clay should be about half an inch thick.

2 Use the pencil to make a pattern in the clay. Keep the lines about an inch or more apart. Make lots of twists and turns and a start and a finish. Make sure to add some dead ends, as well.

3 Pressing firmly, roll the marble along the penciled lines to create an indented trough. Let the clay dry overnight.

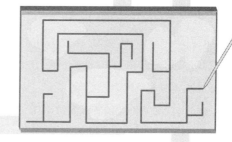

4 To use the labyrinth, place the marble at the starting point and see if you can roll it all the way from the beginning to the end.

activity: Ancient Greek-opolis

Ancient Greek-opolis

a perilous trip through ancient Greece

Design your own perilous trip through ancient Greece!

1 Use a pencil to lightly draw the game board and the path that players will travel. You'll need a start and finish line, and lots of square spaces in between. You can make the path square or create a spiral—it's your choice.

2 When you are happy with the layout of the board, use markers to make the path permanent and to decorate the board (not the spaces) with Greek designs. Color some of the spaces on your board to match the colors of your index cards. Leave some spaces blank.

3 Cut 10 index cards of each color in half. On one color of cards, write a true or false statement relating to ancient Greece. Include the answer on the card. Here are a few to get you started:

- Medusa's hair was made of worms (F)
- *Polis* means city-state (T)
- Athens and Sparta were *poleis* in ancient Greece (T)

4 On the rest of the cards, write down some fun (or funny) things that might happen to an ancient Greek along with instructions that will move a player forward or backward:

- Found innocent by a jury of your peers; move forward 2 spaces
- Decipher the Linear A tablets; take an extra turn

5 Players take turns rolling the dice and moving their marker accordingly. If you land on a color, choose a card to match and follow the directions. If you pick a True or False card, answer the question; if you are correct, move two spaces forward. If not, move back two spaces. The first person to cross the finish line wins.

supplies

- ☒ **poster board or cardboard**
- ☒ **pencil**
- ☒ **colored markers**
- ☒ **index cards** in three different colors
- ☒ **2 dice**
- ☒ **buttons** for markers

BIBLIOGRAPHY AND RESOURCES

Archibald, Zofia. *Discovering the World of the Ancient Greeks.* New York: Facts on File, 1991.

Boardman, John; Griffin, Jasper; Murray, Oswyn. *Greece and the Hellenistic World.* New York: Oxford University Press, 1992.

Burrell, Roy. *The Greeks.* New York: Oxford University Press, 1990.

Clare, John D. (editor). *Ancient Greece.* Orlando, FL: Harcourt Brace, 1993.

Davis, William Stearns. *A Day in Old Athens.* Cheshire, CT: Biblo-Moser, 1960.

Garland, Robert. *Daily Life of the Ancient Greeks.* Westport, CT: Greenwood Press, 1998.

Gilbert, Adrian. *Going to War in Ancient Greece.* Danbury, CT: Franklin Watts, 2001.

Greenblatt, Miriam. *Alexander the Great and Ancient Greece.* New York: Benchmark Books, 2000.

Hart, Eloise. "The Delphic Oracle." *Sunrise magazine*, October/November 1985. Theosophical University Press.

Nardo, Don. *Life in Ancient Athens.* San Diego, CA: Lucent Books, 2000.

Nardo, Don. *Life in Ancient Greece.* San Diego, CA: Lucent Books, 1996.

Pearson, Anne. *Ancient Greece.* New York: Alfred A. Knopf, 1992.

Philip, Neil. *Myths and Legends.* New York: DK Publishing, Inc. 1999.

Philip, Neil. *Mythology of the World.* Boston: Kingfisher Publications, 2004.

Powell, Anton. *Ancient Greece, Cultural Atlas for Young People.* Oxford, England: Equinox, 1989.

Encyclopedia Mythica—http://www.pantheon.org/areas/mythology/europe/greek/articles.html

Hellenic Ministry of Culture—http://www.culture.gr/2/21/211/21101a/e211aa03.html

Metropolitan Museum—http://www.metmuseum.org

Minnesota State University Mankato—http://www.mnsu.edu/emuseum/information/biography/pqrst/schliemann_heinrich.html

The Perseus Project/tufts—http://www.perseus.tufts.edu/

Technology Museum of Thessaloniki—http://www.tmth.edu.gr/en/aet/1/13.html

Washington State University—http://www.wsu.edu

MSN Encarta, 2003

http://www.physlink.com/Reference/GreekAlphabet.cfm

http://www.egypttourism.org/New%20Site/places/bibliotheca_alexandrina.htm

http://www.bookrags.com/notes/od/BIO.htm

GLOSSARY

acropolis: high place of the city.

agora: open-air market.

alliance: a group whose members agree to help each other.

altar: a raised table or structure where religious ceremonies take place.

analog computer: a device that uses mechanical methods to model a problem.

anarchy: a chaotic period with no clear leader.

anatomy: the branch of science that studies the body.

apprentice: someone training for a profession.

archaeologist: someone who studies the tools, buildings, graves, and other objects of people who lived in the past to learn about their culture.

archaic: from a much earlier period of time, the earliest phases of a culture.

archon: after the age of kings, city-states were ruled by nine archons.

Areopagus: a council of nobles beneath the king.

arid: very dry, with little rainfall.

artifact: an object made by a human, usually a tool or ornament, that has survived from a long time ago—an artifact is a kind of relic.

astronomy: the science of the celestial bodies, like the planets and stars.

Athens: the cultural center of ancient Greece.

atom: the most basic, smallest particle of matter.

Attica: Athens and the surrounding region.

balbis: the starting line.

barbarian: foreigners with an unrecognizable language that sounded to the Greeks like "bar bar."

barter: to trade one thing for another.

basileus: a Greek king.

biology: the science of life.

boule: a government council of 400 men balancing the Areopagus.

bronze: a metal made from a mixture of copper and tin that is very hard.

chorus: singers, dancers, and musicians who acted out the drama, told by a storyteller.

climate: typical weather in an area.

column: a round pillar used to support weight in a building.

comedy: a play that makes the audience laugh by poking fun at politicians, famous people, and even the gods.

constellation: a group of stars forming a pattern or shape.

crop: plants grown for food or other uses.

cuirass: a piece of armor covering the body.

data: factual information

deductive reasoning: the truth of the premises guarantees the truth of the conclusion.

degree: a unit of measurement. There are 360 degrees in a circle.

deity: form of god or higher being.

Delian League: a military alliance of Greek city-states dominated by Athens.

democracy: rule by the people .

diaulos: a footrace roughly 400 meters long.

dolichos: a footrace roughly 4,800 meters long.

dowry: the property that a woman brings to her husband at the time of the marriage.

drama: Greek word meaning "action."

eclipse: when an astronomical object such as the sun or moon is partially or completely blocked from view by another astronomical object.

ekecheiria: the Greek word for truce, literally means "holding of hands."

export: to sell to another country.

fermentation: a process where something breaks down into a simpler substance.

frieze: a carved band around a building.

geocentric: from the perspective of the earth as the center.

geography: the science of the earth and its features.

geometry: the measurement and relationships of points, lines, angles, surfaces, and solids, from the Greek geo (earth) and metro (measure).

gymnasium: place to exercise in the nude.

heliocentric: the sun is the center.

hoplite: a foot soldier in ancient Greece armed with a sword and a spear.

hysplex: the starting gate that ensured all runners started at the same time in ancient Greek running races.

impiety: a lack of respect for a god or religion.

import: to buy from another country.

inductive reasoning: the truth of the premises lends support to the conclusion but does not guarantee it.

interpretation: an explanation of the meaning or importance of something.

League of Corinth: a military alliance of all the Greek city-states except Sparta, led first by King Philip of Macedonia and then his son, Alexander. The alliance lasted until Alexander's death in 323 BCE.

legislative bill: the action of proposing a law, an idea for a new law.

logic: the science of formal, correct reasoning.

lyre: stringed instrument.

magistrate: someone who administers laws.

matter: any substance that takes up space.

Marathon: the village where the Greeks won a major battle over the Persians, and a running race of 26 miles, 385 yards (42.195 kilometers).

mechanics: a branch of physical science that studies energy and forces in relation to solids, liquids, and gases.

mint: to make coins.

molten: a liquid, created by melting with heat.

monopoly: to control all of something in a market.

mortal: someone who can die—the opposite of immortal, like gods, who cannot die.

mythological: imaginary.

oligarchy: rule by a few.

oracle: a source of wisdom or knowledge.

orchestra: the stage area used by the chorus.

Panathenaea: an Athenian festival held in mid-August celebrating Athena's birthday.

Panhellenic: all Greek.

Panhellenic Cycle: a series of four religious and cultural festivals.

pankration: unarmed combat combining hitting and wrestling with very few rules.

pantheon: a group of gods, heroes, or important people all considered collectively.

parallel: side by side, always the same distance apart.

peer: a person who is of equal standing with another in a group: your friends are your peers.

Peloponnesian League: a military alliance of Greek city-states dominated by Sparta.

Peloponnesian War: wars between the Greek city-states of Athens and Sparta that weakened both powers.

pentathlon: a series of five events including discus, long jump, running, javelin, and wrestling, from the words penta, meaning "five," and athlon, meaning "contest."

periodonikes: the Greek work for circuit winner. From the words peri and hodos, meaning "going around in a circle," and Nike, the goddess of victory who presided over all athletic and military contests.

Persian Wars: a series of wars between Persia and the Greek world between 499 and 449 BCE.

phalanx: rows of soldiers marching tightly together with their shields joined.

philosophy: a quest for truth through logical reasoning, from the Greek word meaning lover of wisdom.

polis: city-state (plural poleis).

premise: a condition stated at the beginning, something assumed.

properties: a quality or feature of something.

prophecy: a prediction of a future event.

prophet: someone who claims to be the voice of god, or who predicts the future.

purify: to clean, make something pure.

physics: the scientific study of matter, energy, force, and motion, and the way they relate to each other.

quarry: where marble and rock is cut from the earth.

relic: something that has survived from a long time ago.

rhapsodoi: poetry performed as a story, often to music.

ritual: a set of formal actions repeated in a ceremony.

rivet: a short metal fastener.

sacred: something very special, worthy of worship.

sacrifice: to offer something of value to a god.

scaffolding: a temporary platform supported by a framework or suspended by rope that allows work at a great height.

science: the study of the physical and natural world using observation and experiment.

scientific method: a system of gaining knowledge in a scientific way by formulating a question, collecting data through observation and experiment, and testing a theory or possible answer to the question.

Socratic method: a way of finding the truth through a series of questions.

Sparta: a warlike city-state in ancient Greece.

Spartan: someone from Sparta. The word has come to mean simplicity, avoidance of comfort and luxury, and strict self-discipline.

sphere: a globe or object similar in shape to a ball.

stade: 200-meter distance.

stadion: a short footrace, roughly 200 meters long, named after the building it was held in.

strait: a narrow channel of water connecting two larger bodies of water.

supernatural: magical or relating to a god.

terraced: strips of level land cut into a hillside.

terra-cotta: a hard, semi-fired, waterproof ceramic clay used in pottery and building construction.

theory: an idea about something, that explains why something is the way it is.

trade: exchanging one thing for another.

tragedy: a play that usually depicts events from a mythical past and that often ends sadly.

trance: in a dazed or hypnotized state, unaware of the surroundings.

worship: to show great devotion and respect, to pray.

zoology: the science of animals, a branch of biology.

INDEX